OXFORD CHILDREN'S REFERENCE LIBRARY

INDIA AND HER NEIGHBOURS

OXFORD CHILDREN'S REFERENCE LIBRARY
General Editors: Patrick Moore and Laura E. Salt
Illustrations Editor: Helen Mary Petter

1
THE UNIVERSE
By COLIN RONAN
Illustrated by David A. Hardy

2
EXPLORING THE WORLD
By PATRICK MOORE
Illustrated by Joan Williams and Clifford Bayly

3
ANIMALS
By MAURICE BURTON
Illustrated by Edward Osmond

4
INDIA AND HER NEIGHBOURS
By TAYA ZINKIN
Illustrated by Biman Mullick

5
STORIES OF COURAGE
By CLEODIE MACKINNON
Illustrated by Peter Branfield

6
THE EARTH
By JEAN PETRIE
Illustrated by David A. Hardy

7
RUSSIA AND HER NEIGHBOURS
By LOVETT EDWARDS

Oxford Children's Reference Library

4

INDIA AND HER NEIGHBOURS

by
TAYA ZINKIN

illustrated by
BIMAN MULLICK

OXFORD UNIVERSITY PRESS
1967

Oxford University Press, Ely House, London W.1

GLASGOW NEW YORK TORONTO MELBOURNE WELLINGTON
CAPE TOWN SALISBURY IBADAN NAIROBI LUSAKA ADDIS ABABA
BOMBAY CALCUTTA MADRAS KARACHI LAHORE DACCA
KUALA LUMPUR HONG KONG TOKYO

© *Oxford University Press 1967*

PHOTOTYPESET BY BAS PRINTERS LIMITED, WALLOP, HAMPSHIRE
PRINTED IN GREAT BRITAIN BY JARROLD AND SONS LTD., NORWICH

Contents

		Page
	INTRODUCTION	6
1	THE SUB-CONTINENT OF INDIA	8
2	THE ANCIENT PEOPLE OF INDIA	10
3	THE STORY OF RAMA AND SITA	12
4	THE MAHABHARATA	14
5	THE CASTE SYSTEM	16
6	THE BUDDHA	18
7	INDIA'S GOLDEN AGE	20
8	THE RAJPUTS	22
9	THE MUSLIMS INVADE INDIA	24
10	THE EMPIRE OF BABUR AND AKBAR	26
11	INDIA UNDER THE MOGUL EMPERORS	28
12	THE EAST INDIA COMPANY	30
13	ROBERT CLIVE	32
14	RAM MOHAN ROY AND THE MUTINY	34
15	BRITISH INDIA	36
16	GANDHI, THE LEADER OF INDIA	38
17	REPUBLIC DAY	40
18	THE MONSOON	42
19	WILD LIFE OF THE JUNGLE	44
20	VILLAGE LIFE IN INDIA—1	46
21	VILLAGE LIFE IN INDIA—2	48
22	SANGANEER, A RAJASTHAN VILLAGE	50
23	GANGATIA, A BENGAL VILLAGE	52
24	NAYAGAON, A VILLAGE IN THE PUNJAB	54
25	THE RIVER GANGES	56
26	CHOTAGAON, A VILLAGE IN THE DECCAN	58
27	NADE, A VILLAGE IN KERALA	60
28	MODERN INDIA	62
29	THE CITIES OF INDIA	64
30	THE REPUBLIC OF PAKISTAN	66
31	PATHANS OF THE NORTH-WEST FRONTIER	68
32	THE RIVER INDUS	70
33	A VILLAGE IN WEST PAKISTAN	72

34	A VILLAGE IN EAST PAKISTAN	74
35	RICE AND JUTE	76
36	NEPAL AND THE HIMALAYAS	78
37	THE VALLEY OF KATMANDU	80
38	CEYLON	82
39	A TEA PLANTATION IN CEYLON	84
40	BURMA AND ITS PEOPLE	86
41	THE TEAK FORESTS OF BURMA	88
42	PHEK, A BURMESE VILLAGE	90
43	THE RIVER IRRAWADDY	92
	INDEX	94

Introduction

INDIA AND HER immediate neighbours—Pakistan, Nepal, Burma, and Ceylon—have a great deal in common. For one thing, until they all became independent countries not so very long ago, they were part of the British Empire; and India, Pakistan, and Ceylon are still members of the British Commonwealth of Nations. So all these countries have closer ties with Britain than many parts of the world, although they are a long way away. One would be more likely, for example, to find people able to speak and read English in India or Ceylon than in China or the countries of South America, or in many parts of Europe. Although all these countries have become independent only recently, they have old histories, especially India and Pakistan, and all, except West Pakistan, have been influenced by the teaching of the Buddha (see Chapter 6).

India and her neighbours are all monsoon countries, that is, they depend on the monsoon rains for growing their crops (see Chapter 18). They are mainly farming people with not very many big industries, and they grow and eat cereals, mainly rice. Compared with the people of countries such as England and France, the people of these countries are very poor and do not all get enough to eat, especially if the monsoon rains fail. This is mainly because there are too many people per square mile for countries which have to grow their own food. As these are all hot countries, people wear very simple clothes—mainly strips of cloth wrapped round their bodies. But today, especially in the cities, many people wear European clothes.

As India is far the biggest, the greater part of this book is about India; and as the majority of people live in villages, many of the chapters in this book describe what life in a village is like in different parts of the country. There are chapters about the history, and about the great men, such as Ashoka and Akbar and Gandhi, who have helped to make their history, and there are descriptions of the big rivers, the Himalaya mountains, and the wild animals of the jungle. This book also gives some of the traditional stories or legends of the Hindu people, which are often celebrated in local festivals and holidays.

1 The Sub-Continent of India

INDIA, WITH PAKISTAN and Nepal to the north, Burma to the east, and Ceylon in the south, makes up such a big piece of the continent of Asia that it is often called the sub-continent of India. All these countries are separated from the rest of Asia by a barrier of high mountains, which includes the highest mountain range in the world (see Chapter 36). These mountains run in a great circle from the north-west to the north-east. In the west they separate Pakistan from Persia and Afghanistan. They begin to grow very high in Kashmir, and then they become the great Himalayan Range, which separates northern India, Nepal, and Assam from Tibet, a mountainous country governed by India's great neighbour, China. The mountains run on southwards on the east side of Burma, separating Burma from the countries of south-east Asia.

The sub-continent of India stretches southwards into the Indian Ocean, and the southernmost tip of Ceylon is not very far north of the Equator. So all these countries have what we call a tropical climate. Apart from one area of desert in West Pakistan and North India, there is a great deal of rain in the wet season, mainly from June to October. In the beautiful island of Ceylon, in part of Burma, and in north-east India and East Pakistan, there is very heavy rainfall. There are thick tropical forests and swamps, and the atmosphere is so hot and wet that even steel rusts unless it is well looked after. In other parts, for instance, in Central India, the land becomes baked hard by the hot sun in the months before the rainy season (see Chapters 24, 26), and except during these months water is precious.

There are many great rivers in the Indian sub-continent, which rise in the mountains and play an important part in the lives of the people. Both the Indus and the Ganges rise in the northern Himalayas: the Indus (see Chapter 32) flows south-westwards through West Pakistan, and the Ganges (see Chapter 25) flows south-eastwards. The Brahmaputra and the Irrawaddy rise in the north-eastern mountains, the Brahmaputra flowing through East Pakistan, and the Irrawaddy (see Chapter 43) through the centre of Burma.

In a part of the world which is hot, has big rivers, and mountains, forests, open country, and villages rather than big towns, there are a great many wild animals which we are accustomed to see only in zoos. There are wild as well as domesticated elephants; there are tigers and leopards, rhinoceroses and wild pigs, wild goats and sheep in the mountains, crocodiles in the rivers, and monkeys and snakes everywhere (see Chapter 19). In many parts, especially Ceylon, there are brilliantly coloured birds, such as parakeets and flamingoes. The trees and flowers on the lower slopes of the Himalayas are famous, especially the alpine flowers, rhododendrons, and orchids. And there are some of the largest and most gaudy butterflies and moths in the world.

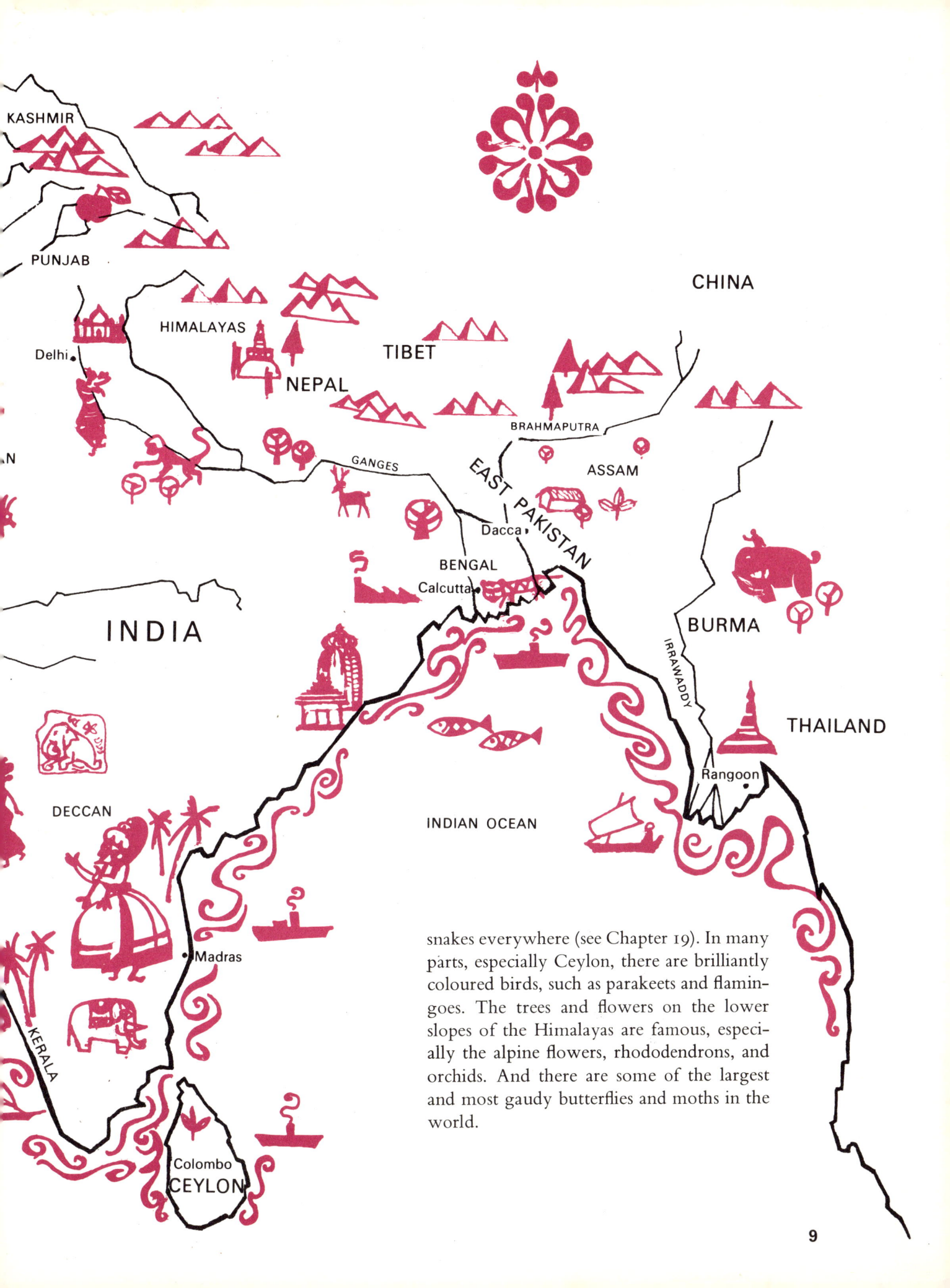

A model of a cart found in a tomb at Mohenjodaro

A statuette found at Mohenjodaro

2 The Ancient People of India

THE EARLIEST PEOPLE of India about whom we know anything lived 4,000 to 5,000 years ago in the fertile valley of the river Indus. This is now in the country we call Pakistan. They learned to live a civilized life in their river valley, as did the ancient Egyptians in the valley of the Nile and the Sumerians in the valley of the Euphrates and Tigris.

These people lived in the Indus Valley for about 1,000 years. Then we hear no more of them; why, we do not know for certain. Possibly a great flood swept over their cities and drowned them, or more likely fierce enemies came down from the mountains and slew them and laid their cities in ruins. Whichever happened, the dust of the desert and the mud of the river gradually moved over the ruins and buried them, until nothing was to be seen at all. For centuries no one knew they had ever existed. Then about 1920, when engineers were digging in the Indus Valley, they came on traces of buried cities. So archaeologists set to work, and bit by bit they cleared away the sand and silt and uncovered again all that remained of the ancient cities, the people, and their possessions. Things which are buried in the sand are often preserved, and archaeologists, by studying carefully all that they found, have been able to learn much about the ancient people of the Indus.

One of the cities of the Indus Valley is called Mohenjodaro, which means 'mound of the dead'. It was built of bricks. A high brick wall surrounded it to protect the people both from enemies and from river floods. Inside there were wide straight streets and brick houses, many of two storeys or more. The houses were often built in a rectangle with a little garden in the middle.

Even those of the poorer people had proper drains built in the thickness of the walls and a supply of running water; and the bigger houses had staircases, lavatories, and bathrooms. There were many public baths for those who did not have private ones, one of which was as big as a large open-air swimming pool. There were temples and a shopping centre and granaries for storing safely the wheat and barley from the country.

The houses had wooden furniture—chests, beds, and seats, and large pottery jars for storing things in. The people were skilled potters, using the potter's wheel and painting the pots with patterns, often in black on a red background. They also wove cloth, and they made beautiful gold, silver, and copper ornaments decorated with precious stones. There were sculptors in Mohenjodaro who made statuettes in copper and marble representing gods and goddesses, especially the mother goddess on whom everything depended for life. They also made figures of animals, particularly bulls, goats, snakes, and crocodiles, which were sacred animals and were often painted bright colours.

In Mohenjodaro have been found a great many little square pieces of carved ivory or pottery, which were seals. Each person had his own seal, as important people in England used to have their own crests. There is a kind of writing on the seals which no one has yet found out how to read. Some day it will be discovered, and then we shall learn much more about these interesting people.

In the countryside the peasants grew grain crops and kept domestic animals. They had dogs, poultry, goats, sheep, and cattle, and they were among the first people in the world to make carts with wheels, with which they could bring their crops into the city, pulled by the big humped bullocks, which are still important beasts of burden in India. They made tools with bronze and copper, metal fish-hooks, sickles, and knives.

In these ancient times there were great forests in the Indus Valley. The people cut down the trees for building and also for stoking the kilns in which they baked their bricks. They cut down more and more trees without planting new ones, until after many hundreds of years the forests had gone. Trees are needed both to hold the soil from being blown away and also to bring the clouds and rain. So the climate changed, and the Indus Valley grew less fertile, and the people became poorer. So we can imagine the people of Mohenjodaro did not bother to make their bricks so well or to repair their city walls against enemies or floods. They did not bother to have well-trained soldiers. Then perhaps one terrible night some 3,500 years ago, disaster came to the people of Mohenjodaro, either by flood or by the attack of an enemy army, we do not know which. Their city was destroyed, and men, women, and children were killed.

There were other cities in the Indus Valley, especially another great city called Harappa on one of the branches of the river Indus. But none of them survived. All were buried in the sand.

A pottery seal (enlarged 3 times). The bull and lettering were cut into the background and made a raised picture when the seal was pressed into soft clay

3 The Story of Rama and Sita

EVERY INDIAN CHILD knows the story of Rama and Sita. This story is more than just a legend; it is like the story of Noah and the Ark: the ideas in it are true, even though the facts may not be. Many Indian parents today call their children after Rama or Sita, the noble prince and his beautiful wife who, in the story, lived 3,000 or 4,000 years ago in the forests by the banks of the river Ganges.

Every year, to commemorate the story of Rama and Sita, there is a big carnival in Northern India, the Ram Lila festival, in which gigantic puppets play the story of Rama and Sita, and which ends in the burning of the demon Ravana, to show how good triumphs over evil.

The good king Rama and his wife, the Princess Sita, lived very happily together in a hut in the midst of the great forest, surrounded by friendly animals and beautiful flowers. Whenever Rama had to go away to look for food he would trace a magic circle round the hut, and Sita knew that so long as she remained inside the magic circle no harm could come to her. One day, Rama drew the magic circle as he always did and warned Sita not to step outside. After he had gone, the evil demon Ravana, who was jealous of Rama, happened to pass by the hut. He saw Sita sitting alone on the grass in front of the hut, playing with a little squirrel. She was so beautiful that Ravana fell in love with her and made up his mind to carry her away to his island kingdom across the sea and make her his wife.

So he thought of a trick to get Sita out of her magic circle; he changed himself into a golden deer of extraordinary beauty. Sita, who loved all animals, when she saw the golden deer, called it to her side. But the deer kept jumping about, without entering the magic circle, until at last Sita, forgetting about the magic circle, ran after the golden deer. No sooner had she stepped out of the magic circle than the deer disappeared, and instead there stood the horrible demon Ravana with his ten heads and his twenty arms. Ravana caught Sita with his twenty arms and carried her away, despite her screams and the heroic efforts of the squirrel to stop him. He carried her to his magic chariot, and they flew back to the island of

Lanka across the sea, the island which is now called Ceylon.

When Rama came back he found the hut empty and the squirrel crying. 'Where is Sita, little friend?' he asked, and the squirrel told him the terrible news. Rama the great prince began to wail and cry, roaming through the forest in his sorrow, sure that Sita was dead. 'Where is Sita, the apple of my eye, the graceful one?' he cried. 'Where is she whose hair is black like the wing of a raven and whose eyes are fish-shaped? Where is she the spring of my happiness, Sita my beloved?' As he wandered weeping, Tatayu the magic bird landed on his shoulder. 'Weep not, oh prince!' said Tatayu, 'I have news of Sita for you. As I was flying over a lovely garden in the island of Lanka, I heard a voice calling, "Rama, oh Rama, help me, save me!" I looked down and saw Sita, and she called to me to tell you to come and save her before Ravana marries her by force.'

Rama and the animals of the forest held council, and they all decided to go to Lanka to rescue Sita—the monkeys, the deer, the little squirrel, and all the rest. The magic bird Tatayu led the way, flying overhead, and the others followed through the forest until they reached the sea-shore. What could they do now? They could not fly across the ocean as Ravana had done, and there was no boat. Then Hanuman, the king of the monkeys, had an idea. He called to all his monkey people to collect stones from the shore and to bring them to Rama. Rama wrote the name of God on each stone, and this made it light so that it would float on the water like a cork When there were enough magic stones made light with the name of God, the monkey people threw them into the sea to build a floating bridge. The little squirrel, who wanted also to help to rescue his friend Sita, tried to lift a magic stone, but it was too heavy for one so small. The squirrel began to cry, but Rama saw him and stroked his back to cheer him up. This is why Indian squirrels have five white marks on their back, the mark of Rama's fingers. The monkey people worked all day and all night, and by the next day they had built a magic floating bridge to Lanka. Rama and his friends crossed over to Lanka, and Rama challenged the demon Ravana in combat. He killed Ravana and brought Sita back to India with him, where they lived happily ever after.

Today, monkeys are sacred in India because of the help the monkey people gave to Rama and Sita. No one in India will kill a monkey, and Hanuman, the king of the monkeys, is one of the most popular gods of the Hindus. In many places, also, there are carvings of the story of Rama, Sita, and the monkey people.

The monkeys make a bridge of stones to Lanka

4 The Mahabharata

ABOUT 3,000 YEARS ago there were two great kingdoms in the lands of the Ganges River. What we know about these kingdoms comes from an epic story called the Mahabharata. Like Homer's story of the Trojan Wars and, indeed, like many of the Old Testament stories, the Mahabharata was not written down until much later, because the people of that time did not know how to write. In ancient India there were bards whose special task it was to learn such stories by heart and pass them on from father to son very carefully, until such time as they could be written down. We now know that events did happen much as the Mahabharata story tells, for archaeologists digging in that part of India have found evidence which agrees with the story.

The Mahabharata is the story of the great war between the Pandavas and the Kauravas, the kings of these two great kingdoms. Each kingdom was ruled by five brothers. These brothers were all descended from the same grandfather, but the Kauravas were mean and wicked, and the Pandavas were kind and trusting. The Pandavas had one wife between them, whose name was Draupadi. In those days in ancient India it was thought quite right for one woman to have several husbands or one man several wives. Draupadi was a virtuous woman whose whole life was devoted to her husbands.

One day, when the Pandava brothers with Draupadi, their wife, were visiting the Kaurava brothers at their court, the Kauravas invited them to play a gambling game with dice. The Kauravas cheated and loaded their dice, so naturally they kept winning. The Pandavas were too honest themselves to suspect foul play, and so they went on playing. First they lost all their fortune, then they lost their kingdom, and when they had nothing left to gamble away, the Kauravas cried, 'Oh Cousins, throw the dice just once more; if you win you regain your kingdom and your fortune; if you lose we win Draupadi your wife.' Draupadi, who was watching the game, was terrified when she heard this and began to pray to the gods to come to her rescue. The dice were thrown once more, and naturally the Pandavas lost again. The Kauravas had won Draupadi, and immediately they ordered her to come and sit by their side. Draupadi tried to run away, but the angry Kaurava brothers caught hold of her sari—the long piece of cloth Indian women wind round themselves as their main garment—and began to pull. Then the gods performed a miracle. To prevent Draupadi from having her garment pulled off her, they made the sari endless. The more the Kauravas pulled, the more the sari unwound itself, and still Draupadi stood there fully covered.

The Kauravas were so frightened by this miracle that they told the Pandavas that they could keep Draupadi; they said that if the Pandavas all went to live in the forest like hermits for 14 years, then they would give them back their kingdom. The Pandavas went humbly away to the forest, taking Draupadi with them. But when, after 14 years, they came out of the forest to claim their kingdom, the wicked Kauravas refused to give it back and mocked them. So a terrible war started, a war in which all the chieftains and the kinsmen who lived in the Ganges plain had to take sides, either with the Pandavas or with the Kauravas. This great war lasted for a very long time, and many on both sides were killed. But in the end the Pandavas won because theirs was a just cause, and the gods were on their side. They killed all the Kauravas and won back their kingdom, and then they and Draupadi lived

Draupadi's sari grows longer and longer

happily ever after. As all the Kaurava brothers were dead, Draupadi's sons became the sole rulers of India.

Every Indian today learns the story of the Mahabharata, and from it they learn the lesson that evil does not pay. The Kauravas cheated at dice and they did not keep their word; also they showed no respect for women by treating Draupadi so roughly. So they were all killed in the end. The Pandavas who were good were punished also because they had been gambling too much, and because they did not rise to defend Draupadi when the Kauravas tried to grab her. So they had to do penance in the forest for 14 years, and then had to fight a very long war before they could enjoy their kingdom and live in peace. All the stories of the Indian people—the story of Rama and Sita, the story of the Mahabharata, and many others— all show that those who act in an evil way will always suffer the consequences.

5 The Caste System

IN ANCIENT INDIA people were divided into five groups called castes, according to their occupations. The top caste, the most important and respected, was the Brahmin or priestly caste; the next was the caste of soldiers and kings; then came the merchants and craftsmen, such as jewellers; potters, weavers, masons, and peasants who cultivated the land were the fourth caste; and lowest of all came the Outcastes, who were the poorest people, regarded as little better than animals. The Indians believed that each caste was descended directly from a particular part of the body of the supreme Creator. They believed the priestly caste to come from the Head of God, the soldiers and kings from the arms of God, the merchants and craftsmen from God's legs, and the peasants from His feet. The Outcastes, like all the animals, were thought to have a little bit of God in them, but no particular part. Children belonged to the caste of their parents.

In the very ancient days people could change their caste. For example, the son of a soldier who was more fond of reading and praying than of fighting could cease to be a soldier and become a priest. There are many stories of people who changed their caste. For example, King Pandu, the father of the five Pandava brothers we read about in the last chapter, fell in love with the beautiful daughter of an Outcaste fisherman whom he saw when he was out hunting. He married her, and she was able to cease being an Outcaste and become a member of his caste. But as time went on, it became more and more difficult for Indians to change their caste or for a person to marry anyone outside his own caste.

It was the priests who made it more and more impossible for people to change caste. They did not want to share their superior position with other people, and as it was their duty to explain the rules of the world to other people, they began more and more to teach people that priests were above everyone else, and so it was impossible for anyone else to become a priest during his lifetime. But Indians believe that when people die they are born again, perhaps into another caste. Into what caste a person is born depends on whether he behaved well or ill during his previous life. If a soldier behaves well during his lifetime, defending the poor and the oppressed, and killing only because of his duty, he may in his next life be born the son of a priest. But if he behaves badly, he may be reborn as a peasant's son, or an Outcaste, or even a cockroach or a worm. If a Brahmin or priest lives a life of goodness he will be rewarded by not being reborn into the world at all but by returning to God his creator and being at peace.

The priests not only taught the people that they could not change from one caste to the other during their life, but only in the next life; they also taught that priests were to be respected and looked up to. It was against the law to kill a priest, while to give a priest a gift, such as a meal or, even better, a cow or an orchard, was a virtuous action. Priests, for their part, were obliged to lead good lives, to say their prayers regularly, and to help the rest of the people with advice and prayers. If a priest did not behave well, if he lost his temper or was tempted by worldly things, he was sure to be punished in after life, sometimes even in this life.

Every Indian child knows the story of the priest who lost his temper. A very learned and holy priest was sitting under a tree thinking about God. Two birds were flying overhead, and they disturbed his thoughts by letting droppings fall upon his head. The priest looked up into the sky furiously, and such was the power of the holy man's eyes that the anger in them struck the two birds dead, as if they had been hit by arrows. Later that day the priest went to a peasant's hut to beg for his evening meal, as he usually did. 'Wait, oh priest,' said the peasant's wife. 'My husband has just come back from the fields, and I must feed him first.' The priest knew that she was right to attend to her husband before all other duty, so he sat in the courtyard and waited, lost in meditation.

The peasant's wife forgot all about him until, as she was going to go to bed, she heard an angry knock at the door. It was the priest demanding his evening meal. 'Do not get angry, oh venerable priest,' the good woman said; 'remember those poor birds you killed today.' The priest was thunderstruck. 'Oh woman, how do you know about the birds? I was alone in the forest.' And he touched her feet as a sign of respect. The peasant woman smiled and said, 'I know many things; for instance, I know that to be forgiven for your sin of anger you must walk for 30 days until you reach the town which lies far away on the Ganges. There you will find a certain butcher who will tell you what to do.'

The priest humbly took his leave and walked for 30 days to the far-away city and found the butcher who was waiting for him. 'You must go to the mountains,' said the butcher, 'and stay there praying for 14 years, repeating the name of God, and then your sin will be forgiven.' The priest did as he was told.

The interesting part of the story is that the priest, who was an important person of the highest caste, was told how to repent by a peasant woman of a very low caste and by a butcher who was an Outcaste. This shows that it does not really matter what caste you belong to. All that matters is how you behave.

A Brahmin priest. He wears a sacred thread over his left shoulder and a scarf with the word god written on it, and he carries a bowl with flowers and a fan for fanning the statues of the gods

The Buddha leaves his former life

6 The Buddha

ABOUT 2,500 YEARS AGO, more than 500 years before the birth of Christ, there appeared in India a very great man who is always known as the Buddha, which means 'the Enlightened One'. The religion he preached is called Buddhism. The Buddha came at a time when Hinduism, the religion of Hind or India, had lost its original meaning. The priests of Hinduism were becoming proud and selfish and ruled the people for their own advantage. They demanded gifts and sacrifices rather than holiness and kindness. Many Indians were growing dissatisfied.

The Buddha, whose real name was Gautama, was the son of a king of Northern India. There are many legends about him, and we cannot tell how true all these are. According to the stories, his father, who had no children, dreamed one night that he would have a son, and that this son would, on growing up, renounce the world and follow the beggar's life armed with a begging bowl. The king did not like this idea, so when this son, Gautama, was born, he made up his mind to prevent the dream from coming true. So he brought up the young prince in a beautiful palace filled with young and beautiful people and surrounded by a garden filled with flowers, fruit-trees, and singing birds. He allowed nothing ugly, nobody old, sick, or sad to come near the prince. He gave strict orders that whenever Gautama drove through the city, anything which might make him sad should be hidden: beggars and old people were driven off the streets, flowers were strewn on the road, and everybody had to look gay.

One evening, however, Gautama went out into the city in his chariot unannounced. Since nobody knew that he was coming, the city was not prepared to receive him, and so he saw for the first time in his life an old man, a sick man, and a dead man. He saw life as it really was, and he was terribly shocked and confused by what he saw. The world was obviously quite different from what he had thought, and he knew that he must find out what it all meant. He travelled to all the centres of education and talked to the best Hindu teachers of his time; but none of them could satisfy him. At last he realized that he must give up everything, including his beautiful wife and his infant son, and go out, as in his father's dream, with nothing except a beggar's bowl. For years he wandered over Northern India, trying to find out what the world was about, and leading a life of hardship and poverty.

One evening, as he was meditating under a tall tree in a forest, he had a sudden feeling that he saw the truth, that he understood the world. From that moment he became the Enlightened One, and he spent the rest of his life preaching the enlightenment that had come to him so that all might share it. He taught that people should live simply, not wanting riches and power, that they should be kind to each other and to animals, that no one should kill, and that sacrifices and caste were unimportant. The Buddha lived himself in the way that he preached, and he soon had many followers.

One story tells how Gautama went to visit the King of Kosala who had just finished a war with a neighbouring king. The king told Gautama that now that he had finished fighting he was going to enjoy having a rest and leisure. 'What would you do, Sire,' asked Gautama, 'if you were told that a mighty landslide was rolling upon you and your city, and that you could not escape it?' Much surprised, the king answered. 'Live righteously, for there would be nothing else to do!' 'I tell you, Sire,' said Gautama, 'old age and death are rolling in upon you, and there is nothing you can do to escape them. What is there that you can do?' Of course the king could only answer, 'Live righteously'; and this was the teaching that Gautama gave wherever he went.

The Buddha lived until he was 80, and by then his disciples had carried his teaching over much of India. Buddhism remained the most important religion of Northern India for about 1,500 years. Many great Buddhist temples and monasteries were built, particularly those carved out of the rock, such as the temples of Ajanta (see Chapter 7). But today there are few Buddhists in India, though Buddhism is still an important religion in Burma, Ceylon, China, Japan, and several other countries of Asia.

The Buddha meditating under the wisdom tree. He is sitting in what is called the 'Lotus pose', which is good for meditation

7 India's Golden Age

Stone lions from the top of one of Ashoka's pillars

ABOUT 350 YEARS AFTER the Buddha's death, there was a very great Indian Emperor called Ashoka, whose grandfather and father had fought fierce battles to drive enemies out of their country. Ashoka also began his reign by fighting a long and very bloody war in which many thousands of people were killed and thousands more died of disease and starvation. When Ashoka saw all the misery caused by his war, he was shocked, and he took a solemn oath to fight no more. He became a Buddhist and gave up all forms of violence, and he set to work to rule his Empire according to the teaching of the Buddha. Ashoka sent many Buddhist monks to preach Buddhism to other countries in Asia, and he reminded his own people of the Buddha's teachings by setting up pillars of stone in many parts of India; on these he had carved the rules of life which Buddhists should follow. In those days of violence and bloodshed, Ashoka's rule of peace and gentleness was very remarkable.

Ashoka was a strong ruler, as well as being a peace-loving one; but those who followed him were weaker, and India fell back again into constant wars. But by about the fourth century A.D. there were strong rulers again; and this is one of the most splendid periods of India's history.

Many great Buddhist monasteries were built, in which the monks not only tried to follow the Buddha's way of life, but also studied and wrote books and made paintings and sculptures. During this time Indian scholars seem to have been the first to invent the way of counting which we use today. They discovered not only how to count by tens, but also from ten to a hundred and from a hundred to a thousand, and so on.

One of the most famous of the Buddhist monasteries is at Ajanta in Central India. Here, the temples and rooms are in caves carved out of the solid rock. There are twenty-nine caves, on the walls and ceilings of which the monks painted scenes from the life of the Buddha. The monks also carved temples out of the rock and filled them with statues and altars. They thought that the more statues of the Buddha there were, the greater their piety. All the painting and sculpture was of religious subjects, and none of it to do with the lives of the ordinary people.

In some of the caves in Ajanta the monks spent their time writing books, decorating them with lovely pictures and designs and illuminating them with gold. One monk might spend his whole life making one book. Instead of paper, they used flat palm leaves, on which they wrote with small, sharp-pointed instruments called styles. They wrote down all the Hindu traditional stories of Rama and Sita, of the Mahabharata, and many stories of animals in which the animals behave and speak like people; and they wrote all the stories of the Buddha. Other monks wrote books about mathematics and astrology. They wrote on palm leaves in an ancient Indian language, which had quite a different kind of writing from the writing we use.

While the monks were working in the monasteries, the peasants living round the monasteries grew crops to feed both themselves and the monks whom they loved and respected. They also wove and dyed cloth. They made a bright orange cloth for the monks' tunics and lengths of white cotton cloth which the peasants wrapped round their waists and tucked between their legs, much as they do today. They made clay pots which they decorated with simple patterns and fired in little ovens. They made cakes of chopped straw and cow-dung for fuel, just as they do today.

This was a time when everyone had his place in life and his work to do. It was the princes' duty to protect the peasants and give land and riches to the monasteries; the monks said prayers for the princes, blessed them and their children, and settled their quarrels for them.

This was a golden age. But, as happens so often when people are too well-off and happy, the monks began to grow lazy and to neglect their writing and teaching. The princes began to quarrel; and the peasants lost faith in both monks and princes. As people no longer lived according to the Buddha's teaching, they lost respect for Buddhism and turned back to their old Hindu beliefs. Gradually Buddhism vanished from India altogether, and the golden age came to an end.

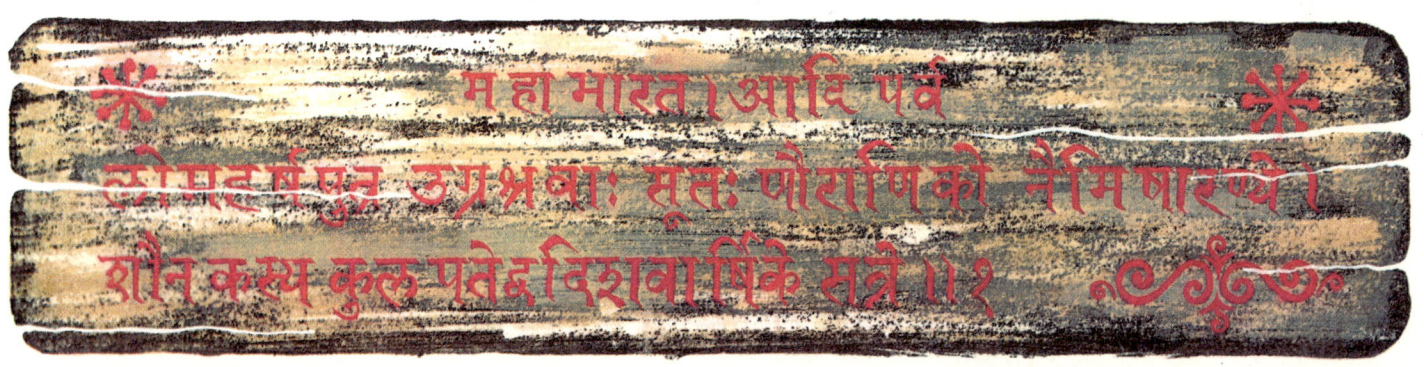

Painting of a ship from one of the caves at Ajanta

The first lines of the Mahabharata written in an Indian script on palm leaves

8 The Rajputs

FROM ABOUT A.D. 900 northern India was ruled by Hindu princes called the Rajputs. The word Rajput means 'son of a king', and the Rajputs claimed that they were descended from the Sun and from the hero-prince Rama. They belonged to the warrior caste, and they were soldiers at heart who loved nothing better than fighting. They fought each other in order to win kingdoms, and when they were not actually at war with each other, they used to fight for pleasure in tournaments, rather as King Arthur's knights did, to prove who was the better horseman and swordsman and to win honour.

They were very much like King Arthur's knights in many ways, for they were fond of hunting, hawking, and pig-sticking, and any manly sport. They would fall in love with some lovely princess and would become her knights errant, wearing her colours and singing her praises. They had many chivalrous ideas, as Arthur's knights had. They respected and protected women and they believed they should protect the poor. After they had been fighting by day, they would call for their bards in the evening to sing ballads, telling of the great deeds of ancient heroes. The ambition of every Rajput prince was to be like one of the heroic Pandava brothers (see Chapter 4), and so the bards sang of these heroes and of the hero Rama. When they were in their camps or castles at night, they would listen to music, watch dancing girls, and make themselves merry by drinking wine or a mixture of milk and opium.

The Rajput princesses used to ride and go hunting with their husbands; some went into battle with them, helping to lead their army against enemies. They were well educated and could read and write in the days when these were rather rare accomplishments. When a Rajput prince died, his

Rajput women singing and playing to a Prince

widow was expected to throw herself on to her husband's funeral pyre and be burned to death with him. This practice is called suttee, and it lasted in some parts of India until not very long ago, when it was forbidden by law. Also if a Rajput prince and his army were defeated, it was the custom for all the ladies of his court to burn themselves to death rather than let themselves be captured by the enemy, who would treat them like slaves. To Rajputs anything was better than dishonour.

During the days of the Rajput princes the people of India were devout Hindus. They would go on long pilgrimages to pray to particular gods; they believed that the gods lived in the mountains or rivers, and so these were favourite places for pilgrimages. To bathe in a sacred river, especially the Ganges (see Chapter 25), was a way of washing away sins. About this time Hindus began to worship cows, though nobody knows how the idea started. Even today no true Hindu will kill a cow even if it is sick, and in those days a man who killed a cow would be put to death himself. Monkeys, as we know, were sacred because they had helped Rama to find Sita, and peacocks were sacred because their many 'eyes' (the marks in their feathers) were supposed to make them able to see everything. There were many gods, such as the favourite elephant-headed god Ganesh who brings good luck; and all these gods of the Rajputs are still worshipped by Hindus today.

The Rajputs built many fine fortified palaces which they placed on the tops of hills so that they could keep a look out for enemies. They also built beautiful shrines dedicated to particular gods. As they were strict Hindus, they allowed the Brahmins (priests) to become powerful, and the rules of caste (see Chapter 5) were very strictly kept.

According to the rules of caste, only the members of the warrior caste were expected to fight. This had the great advantage that the peasants did not have to fight and be killed in their lords' many battles, but could attend to growing their crops. Only the Rajputs themselves were trained to fight, and only they had weapons. And they were so busy fighting among each other that they were not at all ready to combine against an outside enemy. So when fierce powerful enemies came down over the mountains to invade India, there was no large, well-armed, well-trained army to meet them.

Hunting in the time of the Rajputs

9 The Muslims invade India

WHEN THE RAJPUT princes were busy fighting each other, and the monks were growing comfortable and lazy in their monasteries, far away in Arabia a new religion was growing up, whose founder was Mohammed. This religion is called Islam, and its followers are Moslems or Muslims. Mohammed and his followers thought that it was their duty to make everyone believe in their own God, Allah, even if they had to do so by force. Islam was, therefore, a warlike, missionary religion, and Mohammed's followers set out to conquer the whole world and to make the people Muslims. So the Muslims sent out armies east and west, and gradually conquered all the countries which lie between Arabia and India.

At the beginning of the eleventh century, about 60 years before William the Conqueror invaded England, a powerful Muslim prince of Afghanistan called Mahmud of Ghazni made up his mind to invade India. He not only thought it was his duty as a servant of Allah to destroy Hinduism, but also he had heard how rich were the Indian princes and the monasteries and temples. So he took a vow that he would invade India every year.

Every October, Mahmud of Ghazni with a great army of horsemen raided India from the north. He attacked the princes and looted the temples, and then, when the weather began to get too hot in the Indian plains, he and his army returned to the mountains of Afghanistan, loaded with treasure. In one great battle with a Rajput prince, Mahmud's army utterly defeated the prince, took him and all his family and chiefs prisoner, slaying many of them, captured 500,000 slaves and 580 elephants, and ransacked the palace for gold and jewels.

Then one year Mahmud decided to raid the richest of all the temples of India, the Temple of Shiva, one of the chief Hindu gods, which stood on the seashore in northwestern India. A thousand Brahmin priests performed the daily prayers there, and

Muslim invaders

thousands of pilgrims used to come there every year to pray and to bring offerings. The Temple was so well surrounded by fortified walls that the Brahmins did not fear the Muslim invaders. Also they believed that Shiva, the God, would defend his sacred city and his own Temple.

Mahmud of Ghazni set out with 30,000 picked horsemen, rode across the plains for 6 weeks, and then laid siege to the city. After 2 days the Muslims climbed the walls, stormed the city, and easily took it. They slew 50,000 Hindus, destroyed the temple, smashed the statue of Shiva, and carried away all the rich treasure.

At first the Muslims merely raided India and went back to their own cities; but soon they began to settle in India and to make an empire there. They called the land Hindustan. A Muslim general from Afghanistan, who had murdered his lord, set himself up as a Sultan and built himself a capital at Delhi. He was himself murdered by his nephew Ala-ud-din, who was a cruel and strong ruler. Ala-ud-din forced the wretched Hindus to pay him so much money that they had hardly anything to live on. He treated them as little better than animals because they were not Muslims, and he forbade them to have horses, to wear silk clothes or gold and silver ornaments, to drink wine, or to gamble. He sent spies round everywhere, so that no man felt safe to speak to another for fear of being seized and imprisoned. He kept the people so near starvation that they had no strength to rebel. In the meantime Ala-ud-din sent his armies out to defeat the Hindu princes and to conquer the lands farther and farther south. In the end he was murdered himself by one of his own generals.

For 9 years one Sultan after another made himself lord until he in his turn was murdered. Then a very strong and even more cruel general, called Mohammed Tuglak, seized power. He loved magnificence, and wherever he went he was accompanied by gloriously decorated elephants, standards, and canopies sparkling with gold and jewels, and his servants showered gold and silver coins. But his reign was so extravagant and cruel that at last even his own soldiers revolted. A terrible famine fell on the land, and the empire of the Sultans broke up. This was a very sad time for India.

10 The Empire of Babur and Akbar

BABUR WAS A Turk whose father ruled an empire lying north of India. His father died when Babur was only 12 years old. Babur was enormously strong, and a very good rider, archer, swordsman, and swimmer. According to the story, when he was still a boy, he used to run around the fortified walls of his palace, carrying a man under each arm and jumping from one battlement to the other.

When Babur was only 15 he made up his mind to conquer India, because he believed that India was rich. India had, indeed, been very rich, but the Muslim invaders such as Mahmud of Ghazni and the Sultans of Delhi had taken almost all the wealth. So when Babur conquered Delhi he was very much disappointed. 'The people are not friendly,' he wrote in his account of his expedition. 'They have no horses, no good meat, no grapes or melons, no fruits, no ice or cold water, no good food in their bazaars, no baths, no colleges, no good craftsmen.' Babur also found Delhi much too hot for him, so he very soon went back to his own home in Afghanistan. But, though Babur did not stay, his successors stayed in India and established an empire we call the Mogul Empire, with its capital at Delhi in the Indian plain.

The greatest of the Mogul Emperors was Akbar, who succeeded his father as Emperor when he was barely 13 years old. No one would have thought then that Akbar would be a great ruler. He seemed to be very stupid and he refused to learn to read and write. He never did learn to do much more than sign his name. In fact, Akbar was very intelligent and he had a wonderful memory. He could remember anything that had been read to him once. He grew to love literature and paintings, and he was interested in all the religions of the world, not just Islam, his own religion. He also loved music, flowers, gardens, and palaces, and he built many beautiful buildings in his new capital at Agra. Akbar was also a first-class athlete, and he could ride and walk in the blazing sun for a whole day without feeling the strain. He was so strong that he could kill a man with one blow of his fist or a tiger with one blow of his sword. Like most rulers of those days, he loved fighting; but in times of peace he enjoyed playing polo and taming wild elephants.

People remember Akbar in India with some affection because he was the first, and almost the only, Muslim ruler to try to understand and win the affections of his Hindu subjects. Akbar thought that he

Akbar

should look after the welfare of all his subjects, not only those of his own religion. He thought it should be possible for Muslims and Hindus to feel like brothers. First he abolished the tax which Hindus had to pay just because they were Hindus. Then he himself set the example of friendship by marrying a Hindu princess and welcoming his Hindu brothers-in-law at his court. He gave them titles and made them generals in his army. And he encouraged his followers also to marry Hindu princesses, which many of them did.

When, by 1569, he had brought all his large empire under his authority and had crushed all rebellions, he set to work to rule it fairly and efficiently. He would allow no officials to cheat the people, and he made the taxes fair. He had the same weights and measures used all through the country. He had roads built and also schools, and he encouraged art. His police force kept order everywhere so that people could live in safety.

Akbar was growing more and more dissatisfied with Islam, his own Muslim religion. So he invited men of all religions, Hindu, Buddhist, Christian, and others, to come and discuss their religions before him, so that he might judge. Although he could not read, he could easily follow their arguments, and he did not feel satisfied with any of them. He decided to create a new religion, which would unite both Hindus and Muslims. He ordered his people to pray every day 'Allah ho akbar', which means 'God is great'; but soon Akbar began to think it meant 'God is Akbar', and he grew to think of himself as God. After he was dead, everyone soon forgot his religion; but Akbar was a great ruler with ideas which were very unusual in those days.

Akbar's son and grandson who succeeded him soon undid much of his good work. We remember Akbar's grandson, Shah Jehan, however, because he erected one of the most beautiful monuments in India—indeed, in the whole world. This is the Taj Mahal, a magnificent white marble tomb which Shah Jehan had built for his favourite wife, who died in 1632 after giving him fourteen children. The Taj Mahal stands in a garden on the banks of the river Jumna at Agra, the Emperor's capital. It took 15 years to build, and many thousands of craftsmen from all over the Muslim world. The story goes that the architect was executed as soon as he had finished it so that he could never build another tomb as beautiful as the Taj Mahal. Perhaps the Taj Mahal looks most lovely at dawn when the rising sun turns its white marble dome a pale glowing pink.

The Taj Mahal

The Great Mosque in Delhi

11 India under the Mogul Emperors

FOR MORE THAN 200 years India was ruled by the Mogul Emperors who were Muslims, and, except for the good rule of Akbar, this was an unhappy time for India. Today, the Muslims rule Pakistan (see Chapter 30), and India is no longer under Muslim rule.

The Muslims built many splendid palaces, tombs, and mosques in India, such as the Taj Mahal and the Great Delhi Mosque, one of the biggest mosques in the world; and they also brought to India a special way of painting miniatures and book illustrations with fine detail. But they destroyed many of the beautiful Hindu temples because they belonged to people who did not worship Allah, their God. They thought that the Hindu beliefs were to be despised, so they destroyed the Hindu temples, using the stones to make new buildings or to pave roads. Muslims believe it is wrong to make pictures or sculptures of God, or even of human beings, so they destroyed many of the beautiful Hindu and Buddhist statues.

The Hindus suffered very much under the Muslim rulers, who treated them as inferiors and taxed them heavily. Also, except during the reigns of the few strong Emperors, such as Akbar, there was always war, even more than during the time of the Rajput princes. And war brings poverty and famine. Whenever an Emperor died, there were bitter struggles for his throne; and sometimes a prince who hoped to succeed the Emperor would murder those of his relations he thought might be rivals. The Emperors were often so busy protecting themselves from rivals that they could not pay proper attention to ruling the country and keeping order. Members of the Emperor's family and generals often decided to leave the court where they might be murdered and to go and set up kingdoms of their own. Usually the Emperor was not strong enough to prevent them. There were bands of robbers everywhere, with none to check them.

These new rulers in India, who called themselves Sultans, were cruel and treacherous and cared nothing for the welfare of their people. One of the most grotesque was a Sultan of Gujerat in the sixteenth century. He had an immense beard which fell down to his waist, and he made his moustaches grow in the shape of buffalo's horns. He had the appetite of a giant, eating 20 or 30 lbs of food every day, while the people round his gates were dying of starvation. Yet all through his reign he lived in terror that someone would poison him.

Life for women was very hard, and they were little better than slaves. Both Muslims and Hindus believed that women were inferior to men. The Hindus had the cruel custom that a widow should throw herself on her husband's funeral pyre (fire) and be burned to death with him. The Muslims shut their women up behind curtains (the purdah) so that no man except their husbands and near relations might see them. When they went out they had to wear long black robes and veils over their faces. According to the Muslim law, a man may have four wives. Rich Hindus also put their women in purdah; but the very poor could not afford to, for the women did much of the work in the fields.

At the end of the fifteenth century there was a young Hindu called Nanak, who lived in what is now Pakistan. He grew dissatisfied with Hinduism, for most Hindus were ignorant and superstitious, and Nanak thought the caste system wrong and unfair. So he turned to Islam, the religion of the Muslims. But this did not satisfy him either; so he tried to build up a new religion which had the best of both the others. He did not deny the many gods of Hinduism, but he regarded them all as inferior to the one Supreme God, who was not unlike the Muslim Allah. He made many disciples who called themselves Sikhs, or disciples. Nanak died in 1538, but his religion still lives. The 'Golden Temple' at Amritsar in the Punjab is a Sikh temple.

In the seventeenth century the Mogul Emperor Jehangir persecuted the Sikhs and tortured their leader to death. So the Sikhs took to arms and fought for their freedom to worship, and they became very good, well-disciplined soldiers. They have succeeded in keeping their religion right up to the present day. There is now a separate state for the Sikhs, in northern India.

A Muslim woman with her son

Nanak and two of his disciples

12 The East India Company

ON DECEMBER 31ST, 1600 Queen Elizabeth I granted a Royal Charter to a group of 125 London merchants to set up a company for trading with India and the East. Most countries in Europe wanted to trade with India because India and the East Indies produced things which everybody wanted and could not get from anywhere else—particularly spices. People wanted spices to help preserve their food, especially meat, through the winter, and to flavour food. The Portuguese, Spaniards, and Dutch had already set up trading stations in India, and the British and French also wanted their share of the trade.

In 1608 the new East India Company sent Captain William Hawkins with orders to establish a trading post in India. With a small fleet, he sailed all the way round the Cape of Good Hope and reached the west coast of India, north of Bombay. He had to get permission from the Emperor at Delhi to set up his warehouse, so he went to the Emperor's court. The story goes that the Emperor, Jehangir, who was the grandson of the great Emperor Akbar, made a bargain with Captain Hawkins that they should have a drinking contest, and that if Captain Hawkins could drink more wine at one sitting than the Emperor, he could set up his warehouses. They had their contest, and, though both could drink a great deal, the Emperor became helplessly drunk while Hawkins was still quite sober. So Hawkins built the first British trading station in India at Surat north of Bombay. Later, another trading station was set up at Fort St. George, Madras, on the south-west coast, and a third on the Hooghly River near Calcutta in Bengal.

The Indian traders brought their merchandise of brocades and silks, beautiful shawls, jewels, tea, and spices to the British warehouses, where they were stored until the ships could take them to England. The East India Company had soldiers to protect the warehouses from the bandits and robbers who roamed over the land, killing and stealing; and the Company built houses for the soldiers and traders to live in. Soon small towns grew up round the warehouses, and the soldiers kept order and peace there. The

An official of the East India Company with an Indian adviser

Indian traders came to live in the towns, not only to make money from the trade but also because they enjoyed the protection from robbers which the British soldiers gave them. The trading stations grew into flourishing cities, with large Indian populations.

As the East India Company made more and more money from their Indian trade, they bought land in India and kept armies to protect their land. They made laws for all the people who lived on their land, put down bandits, and made treaties with the various rulers of the Indian states. As they grew more and more powerful, some of the weak Indian rulers began to rely on them for keeping order in their states and protecting them from their enemies. Many of the rulers became rulers in name only; the real authority was the East India Company. Under their rule the Indian peasants could live without fear.

But the British were not the only Europeans trading in India. The French were also setting up trading stations and making friends with the Indian princes. The British and the French both tried to build up trade with the Indians. Then, in 1742, war between England and France broke out in Europe, and as a result the British and French traders in India also became enemies. Both began to look for Indian allies, and they began to take sides in the local wars between the Indian princes. They gradually got more and more power over the Indians and controlled a larger and larger part of the country.

The British East India Company was by now almost more concerned with ruling India than trading with her. Although it was still a private trading company, it was becoming more and more like the government of an Empire. The Company divided its lands into three provinces with provincial governors—Bengal, with its capital at Calcutta; Bombay; and Madras. The French also had their important centres, and each hoped finally to drive the other out.

A Sepoy (soldier of the East India Company

13 Robert Clive

IN 1743 A young man called Robert Clive was sent out to India by his father to be a clerk in the East India Company offices at Madras in South India. His father sent Robert to India because he did not know what else to do with him. He was always in trouble at school because, instead of learning his lessons, he led gangs of boys into reckless adventures. He was rude and quarrelsome, and no school would keep him. His father thought he might have more opportunity for adventure in India.

Robert was disappointed to find that his work kept him at an office desk, doing accounts. He grew bored and started looking for adventure instead of sticking to his books. For the first 2 years he was always in trouble for disobeying orders and quarrelling with people, and he was so miserable that he twice tried to commit suicide. He would probably have been sent back to England in disgrace had not an opportunity for adventure come his way.

The French and the English, as we know, were fighting each other in India. When Clive was just 21, the French attacked and captured Madras. Clive and a few friends managed to escape to the British garrison at Fort St. David and joined the army. Clive did well and was soon made a captain. Then news came that a British garrison farther south was besieged, and Clive was allowed to lead a small force to attack the city of Arcot so that the French would have to send troops away from Madras to save Arcot.

Clive's little army of only 500 men and hardly any guns marched through violent rainstorms and thunder to reach Arcot. The Indian army in Arcot, thinking that Clive and his men must be gods to march through the storm unharmed and unafraid, fled in panic, and Clive's army took Arcot without

The Indian Emperor giving the East India Company the right to collect the revenue of Bengal

firing a gun. Immediately they set to work to fortify the town, for they knew the French would soon try to recapture it. Clive won the confidence of the Indians living in Arcot, who began to help them, so by the time the French arrived with a large army, Clive was ready for them. For 53 days the French besieged Arcot, but they failed to take it and lost many men in the attempt.

Clive was a born leader. He led his men to further victories, and in 1752 the French had to agree to make peace. By that time Clive had not only won a great reputation as a soldier but he had also made a large fortune.

Clive went home for 2 years, no longer a disgraced schoolboy, but a famous and wealthy general. Then he came back to India as Governor of Madras. The day that he landed, news came that a powerful Indian ruler called Suraj-ud-Dowlah had captured the city of Calcutta. He treated the British garrison well until some of them behaved very badly. Then, by a mistake, 146 men and women were shut all night into a small dungeon 20 feet square with only one small window, known as the 'Black Hole'. By the morning only 23 were still alive. Clive immediately marched an army from Madras to relieve Calcutta. He recaptured the city and thoroughly defeated Suraj-ud-Dowlah.

About 2 years later Clive, with an army of only 3,200 men and very few guns, again utterly defeated the Indian ruler and his huge army of 50,000 Indians with French gunners at the Battle of Plassey. Suraj-ud-Dowlah, instead of attacking boldly, was frightened and retreated. Clive immediately ordered an attack, and the whole Indian army panicked and fled. Clive won his victory, losing hardly any soldiers at all. This great victory brought an end to the French power in India. Clive at the age of 35 was a national hero and was made a Baron by the British Government.

The end of Clive's life was sad. Many of the East India Company officers were tempted to make money for themselves in India, by taking bribes, by cheating the Indians, and also by taking money which really belonged to the Company. Clive had also made money in these dishonest ways and became extremely rich, though he did not cheat the Company as many were doing. In 1762 Clive was sent back to India as Governor of Bengal with directions to stop such cheating and bring order into the affairs of the Company. He was shocked by what he found and reported that Calcutta had become one of the 'most wicked places in the Universe'. He put things in order and prevented the Company's servants from cheating the Indians; but he made many enemies who accused him also of being dishonest.

Clive was recalled to England and put on trial, a trial which lasted a year. He was so disgusted and depressed at being treated as a thief instead of a hero that he did not wait for the end of the trial but took his own life. A famous historian later described him as a man who had great faults but was also 'truly great in arms and in council'.

Robert Clive

14 Ram Mohan Roy and the Mutiny

IN 1772 A BOY called Ram Mohan Roy was born in Bengal, the son of a well-to-do landlord belonging to the priestly caste. Ram's father was a very pious, old-fashioned Hindu, who followed all the Hindu customs of the day. For instance, he married Ram to a girl when he was still only a child, a usual thing to do in India then. Ram, who had a gift for languages, learnt eight or nine, including English and also Greek and Hebrew, which he learnt so that he could read the Bible in its original language.

As a result of reading the Bible, Ram Mohan Roy began to criticize the Hindu customs which his father followed. Then something happened which shocked Ram very much indeed. His brother died, and according to the Hindu custom of suttee, Ram's sister-in-law was burned alive on her husband's funeral pyre. Ram had to be present when this happened, and it horrified him so much that he left home.

Suttee was one of many old Hindu customs which seem to us very terrible. For instance, babies, especially baby girls, were often killed if there were too many of them. Children were sacrificed to the gods, and no one thought it murder. Also travellers were sometimes seized and strangled as a sacrifice to the goddess of death. But worst of all was the treatment of widows. As children were often married when they were still babies a wife might become a widow when she was very young. If she escaped having to commit suttee, she had so miserable a life she might have suffered less had she been burnt. If she belonged to a high caste she could not marry again, but she had to stay as a sort of slave of her husband's family, where no one cared for her and everyone bullied her.

When he left home, Ram Mohan Roy started to travel about Bengal preaching and writing against suttee. When he was 28, he took a job with the East India Company and began to make English friends, including missionaries. This soon made him anxious to bring English customs and laws to India. He started a college in Calcutta where Indians could learn English, and he wrote articles and made speeches to urge the English to pass laws against such cruel things as suttee.

Then Ram paid a visit to England, where he met the King, attended Parliament, and pleaded with everyone he met to bring English laws and education to India. He made a great impression, but he never saw the result of his work, for he died while he was in England.

The British Government, through the East India Company, began to set up laws in India. They declared that anyone, be he rich or poor, prince or peasant, who killed

Ram Mohan Roy

The capture of Delhi

any other person would be hanged as a murderer. This was difficult for the Indians to accept, especially the old-fashioned ones like Ram's father. The English said that everyone was equal before the law, and that if a prince killed a beggar he would be hanged just the same as would a beggar if he killed a prince. But by Indian custom people were not equal: a priest could never be put to death whatever he did; and a rich prince or soldier would never be brought to justice for killing a poor man.

The high-caste Indians, the priests, princes, and landlords, were very angry. They feared that the British meant to change their way of life and destroy their privileges. It happened that, just at this time, some of the common soldiers in the East India Company's army were also dissatisfied, because they had had no pay and were being sent far from their homes to fight for the British, and because of some new rifles with cartridges which had to have their heads bitten off. The cartridges had grease on them to prevent their getting damp. The Hindu soldiers said the grease was cow-fat which as Hindus they must not touch, and the Muslim soldiers said it was pig fat, which they are forbidden to touch. The high-caste Indians did their best to stir up the soldiers' discontent.

In 1857 some soldiers near Delhi were punished for refusing to use the cartridges, and immediately the men turned on their British officers and murdered them. The mutiny quickly became a serious rebellion. The Indians attacked Delhi and killed many Europeans there, and they besieged other cities. The Indian Mutiny lasted for over a year; but it did not spread very widely, and in the end the rebels were defeated.

The hero of the Indian Mutiny was John Lawrence, who had ruled the Punjab in north India so well that the people loved and trusted him, and remained loyal to him. After the Mutiny was over, the British Government decided that the East India Company should be brought to an end, and that India should become part of the British Empire. In 1863 Lawrence was made Viceroy of India, and he ruled India wisely, as Ram Mohan Roy would have wished.

15 British India

WHEN THE EAST India Company came to an end, India became part of the British Empire. In 1876 Queen Victoria was crowned Empress of India, and she ruled India through her Viceroy who lived in Delhi.

The next 80 years were good years for India. The British Government built schools and colleges, hospitals, roads and railways. They made laws and saw that they were kept both by rich and poor. They treated all people the same, from Brahmins to outcastes. If a priest and an outcaste came into a government office, they were treated equally. If the outcaste came first, he was attended to first. If the priest refused to sit with the outcaste in the waiting room, he had to stand. People were happy to have peace and to be secure, and the princes were happy because the British army and navy defended them.

But the British Government did very little to get rid of the bad customs of Hindu tradition against which Ram Mohan Roy had fought. Suttee had been stopped, but the British were afraid that if they passed laws forbidding child marriages, for example, and the cruel treatment of outcastes, there would be more mutinies. They were afraid to interfere with people's beliefs. But as more and more Indians became educated and went to English schools and universities, they themselves wanted to change these bad customs, and they were discontented that the British Government did not make reforms fast enough.

In particular, educated Hindus were ashamed of the way outcastes were treated. It was thought that a man was defiled if he touched an outcaste, and so they were called Untouchables, and had to live in a separate

An Englishman in a palanquin

36

part of the village or town. They might not stand near other people; and they were forbidden to draw water from the village well. They had to go to the river for water or wait by the well until some kindhearted villager drew water for them. They could do only the lowest kind of work. The Untouchables themselves believed that they were born as outcastes because they had behaved badly in a previous life, and so accepted their punishment meekly.

The educated Indians came more and more to think that only Indians could put these things right, and so they began to demand that the British should leave India to govern herself. But the Government did not think there were yet enough educated Indians to be able to govern properly. The Viceroy began to include more Indians in the Government, but he still refused to pass the laws the Indians wanted nearly fast enough to satisfy them.

When a great many people want to make changes very much, before long a leader is sure to appear. About the year 1914, during the First World War, this leader, Mahatma Gandhi, appeared.

Gandhi was 9 years old when Queen Victoria was crowned Empress of India. He was the son of an Indian official who was a strict Hindu of the merchant caste. Gandhi, like many Hindu children, was married to a little girl when he was only 13. Of course, he was much too young to be a good husband, and later he described how unkind he had been to his little wife, scolding her and sometimes refusing to speak to her for days if she had done what he did not like. His young wife never got angry when he was cruel to her, but if he was very harsh, she would simply refuse to eat at all until he behaved better. Gandhi later said that his wife's way of making him behave better was far more effective than anger and violence would have been; and he used the same way himself later against the British Government.

A Maharajah receiving British guests

When Gandhi was a boy he made great friends with the son of one of his father's servants, who was an Untouchable and did all the humblest work in the house. Gandhi's mother, though she was a saintly woman who was always helping the poor and the sick, was very much distressed when she found Gandhi playing with Ukka, the son of an Untouchable. She would scold him and make him go and wash himself. 'But Ukka is quite clean,' Gandhi would say. 'He is an Untouchable,' would answer his mother. Gandhi, who loved Ukka, made up his mind that he would make it his business when he grew up to free the Untouchables and make them as good as anyone else. He used to call them 'the Children of God'.

16 Gandhi, the Leader of India

WHEN GANDHI WAS 17 years old he went to England to study law. Most people in the small state where his family lived were shocked that a Hindu should go to a foreign country, and when after 3 years he came home, he found no place for him. So, as both his parents were dead, he decided to take a job as a lawyer in South Africa, where many Indians lived. He stayed in Africa for 21 years, and during this time he began his fight for justice. But he never used violence, and taught his many followers to find peaceful ways of fighting injustice.

In 1914, at the beginning of the First World War, Gandhi came back to India. By that time he was famous for his non-violent resistance to injustice and was welcomed as a leader. He was convinced that India would never get rid of dreadful things like child marriages and cruel treatment of the Untouchables under British rule. He was sure that only an Indian could lead the Indians to change their customs. Soon he had many devoted followers, who called him 'the Mahatma', which means 'the Great Soul'. Now, he is always called Mahatma Gandhi.

Gandhi knew that if he were to lead his country to freedom he must understand the people of India, and since most of the people in India were poor peasants, he must get to know them by living with them. So he gave up his fine clothes, ate plain food, and went about bare-chested and bare-legged, with just a cheap piece of cotton cloth wrapped round him. He started to tell people to make their own things instead of buying British goods. In particular, he made all his followers learn how to spin and weave their own cloth, instead of buying cloth sent from England. Gandhi took a spinning wheel with him wherever he went.

Then Gandhi told people to make their own salt from seawater instead of buying salt from the Government. According to the law, only the Government might make salt; but Gandhi told the people to disobey the law. He announced he was going to walk to the sea from his home, a journey of about 4 weeks, and make his own salt there. The Viceroy did not take him very seriously, saying, 'Mr. Gandhi thinks he can upset us with a pinch of salt!' But Gandhi's pinch of salt was more powerful than the Viceroy thought. Thousands of people all over India started to walk to the sea to make salt! The Government ordered them not to, but they paid no attention, and it was not possible to put them all in prison for there was not enough room. All they could do was to put Gandhi in prison. Gandhi did not mind being in prison; he said it gave him a chance to make up for lost sleep. Altogether he spent 2,089 days in prison during his life.

In 1932 Gandhi went to England to discuss with the British Government how India should become independent. Even now, he still wore his peasant's clothes. When he went to Buckingham Palace to visit the King, he dressed just the same, with his chest and knees bare. Many people were shocked and thought he looked very odd with his big, closely shaven head, big ears, round spectacles, and strong brown legs. A friend called him 'the Mickey Mouse of India', and this made him laugh, for he had a great sense of fun. He made many friends in England, especially little boys and girls in the streets in the East End of London where he often met very poor families. He was very fond of children.

The British Government agreed that India should become independent, but not as quickly as Gandhi and the Indians wanted. So Gandhi encouraged his followers not to help the British in the Second World War. He was put in prison several times, and there he did what his little wife had done when they were children—he refused to eat. The British did not dare let him die because he was worshipped by the mass of the people. So they had to release him when he got very weak.

After the war the British decided to leave India. But this was not easy either. In northern India particularly, a great many of the people were Muslims, and they did not want to be ruled by the Hindus. So at last, much against Gandhi's wishes, the separate Muslim State of Pakistan was created. There was much bitter fighting between Hindus and Muslims. Gandhi, who believed no one should ever fight, went from one trouble-spot to another, and declared that he would not eat again until the fighting ceased. Neither police nor soldiers had been able to stop the fighting, but Gandhi's hunger strike inspired them to make peace. Then a tragic thing happened. Gandhi, who had all his life preached peace, was murdered by a member of a violent group of Hindus who thought that he was betraying his own people.

Today India is a free country, and the Indian Government has forbidden child marriages and will punish anyone who treats an Untouchable differently from anyone else. Many Hindus are beginning to think less of caste and to believe that people are equal.

Gandhi. He was called 'Mahatma', which means 'Great Soul'

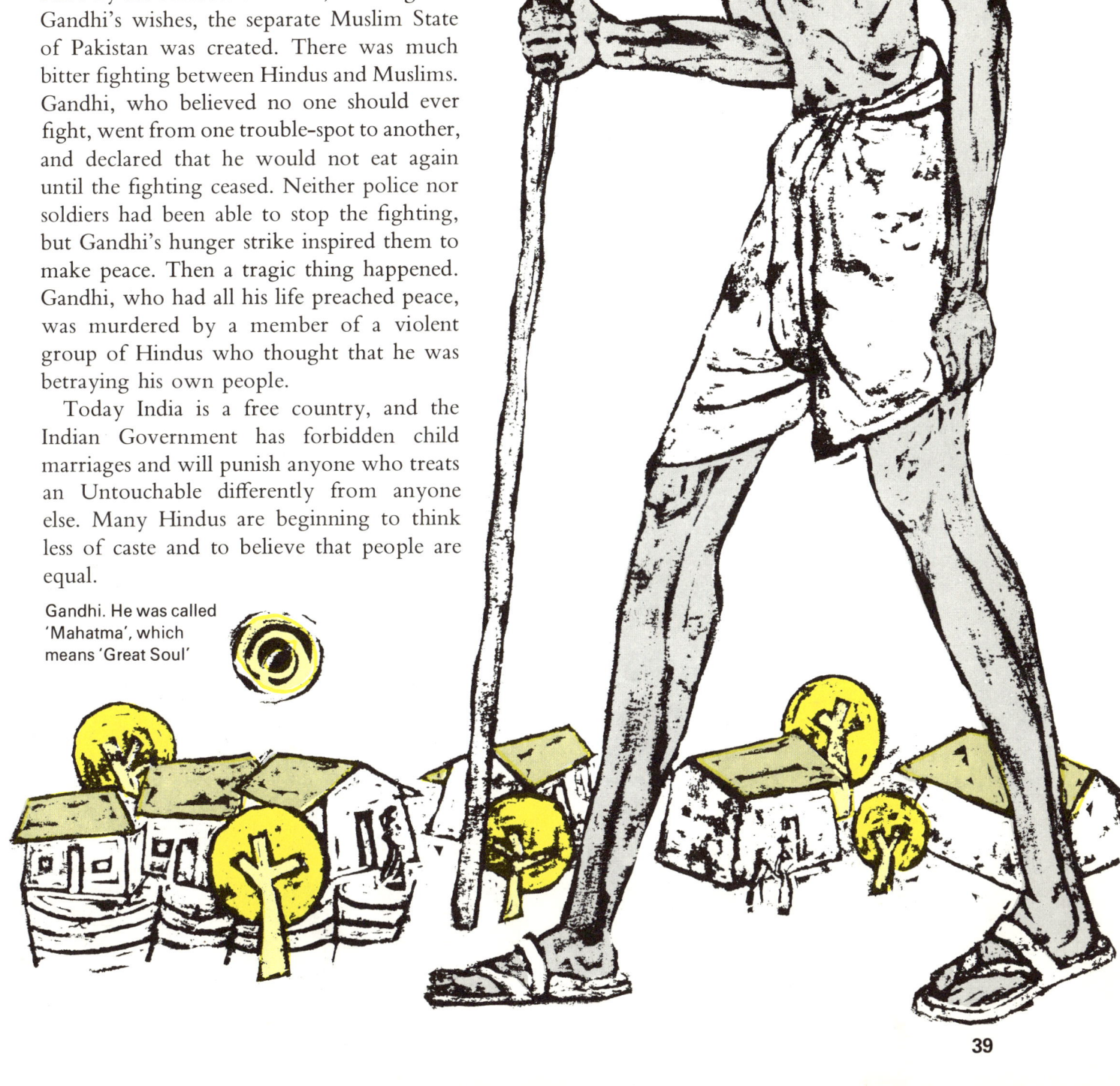

17 Republic Day

EVERY YEAR, ON the 26th of January, the Indian people have a public holiday to celebrate the day India became an independent Republic within the British Commonwealth. Millions of people come in from the countryside to the big cities to take part in the fun and admire the parades. They come on foot, on bicycles, by bullock carts, camel carts, motor-cars, buses, and trains. So many people come that the streets are choked, and it is almost impossible to move.

The largest crowds and the most splendid processions are in Delhi, the Capital. People come not only from the neighbouring countryside but from all over India. Parties of school children are brought from all the States of the Indian Union, and also members from the tribes living in the distant jungles and high mountains come to watch and to take part in the great parade. There is, perhaps, no more impressive national day anywhere in the world.

The long drive from the palace where the President of the Indian Republic lives is lined with thousands of people. They sit on the ground tightly packed together, children and babies and all, and many of them have been sitting the whole night to make sure of getting a good place.

First the President arrives in a grandly decorated open carriage drawn by magnificent horses. Above his head is held a huge velvet umbrella of crimson and gold, just like those the Mogul Emperors used to have. When he reaches the platform, there is a salute of guns, and the President mounts the platform and takes his place so that the procession can march past him—a procession which takes the greater part of the day.

First come the sailors, soldiers, and airforce with their military bands; then the tanks and the armoured cars, with the jet fighters and bomber aircraft overhead. Then come the mounted Camel Corps with their

The Republic Day procession in Delhi

magnificent uniforms glittering in the sun. Next is perhaps the most splendid of all, Rajputs in grand robes and turbans, riding their elephants. The elephants are painted with lovely clear colours, and their trunks and sides are decorated with shining bright armour. On the head of each elephant rides his mahout (or driver), and he proudly holds the Rajput's standard. As he passes by the President he dips the standard in salute, while the elephant salutes with raised trunk.

After the Rajputs come the decorated floats (or platforms on wheels), one for each of the different States of the Indian Union; there is a prize for the best float, and each State tries to show on its float something special about that State. For instance, on one float there may be a model of an ancient temple and of a modern steel mill, with people dressed in the special dress of the State, singing songs in the State's own language and dancing traditional dances, while the float moves slowly along in the procession. As well as the States' floats, there are special floats belonging to schools or colleges or industries. There may be, for example, a float representing an oil refinery, or one to show railway workers making trains, or one for the Cadet Corps of the Indian Army, with young Cadets in uniform parading up and down.

After the floats come bands of boy scouts, girl guides, factory workers, and others; and then at the end come the picturesque tribal dancers and their musicians, who are one of the most popular sights of the parade. When the parade is over, these dancers stay in Delhi for a week and dance every evening in the Stadium so that everyone can see them.

This great procession shows the people of India that their country is very large, with many peoples, many ways of life, and many languages. Republic Day is the one day in the year when all these peoples of India come together in one great celebration and remember that they all belong to each other. In the evening, after the sun has set, they all sit out long into the night watching the wonderful fireworks and illuminations. Then, their great annual holiday over, they all set off in their different ways to go back to their homes and ordinary lives.

18 The Monsoon

A woman offering a coconut to the sea to welcome the rain

THOSE OF US who live in countries where it rains at frequent intervals and in moderate amounts cannot imagine what rain means to the people of countries such as India, Pakistan, Ceylon, or Burma, where the whole of life depends upon whether and where it rains, and on how much it rains. We take water for granted, but to the people of Asia it is a gift from heaven. They worship the rain itself, and also the rivers and the lakes, for without rain their crops would not grow, and they would die. So in India when the rain comes after a long time without any rain at all, people welcome it with celebrations. Those living near the sea, for example, throw offerings of floral garlands and coconuts into the sea.

The Indian word for the rainy season is 'monsoon', but it is also used to describe the torrential rain itself which falls in many parts of Asia during the monsoon season. The monsoon varies from one place to another; in some places there are two monsoons—in the spring and the autumn; but in most countries of Asia there is only one rainy season which lasts from June to the end of October.

If the monsoon is late, the peasant cannot plough his fields, for the earth is baked too hard and dry. If he cannot plough, he cannot sow his seeds. If, when the monsoon comes, the rain is too violent and there is too much of it, his seeds will be washed away, and the village will be flooded. Sometimes, when the monsoon rains are very violent, the rivers flood and destroy whole villages with great waves of flood water. The peasant, his family, his hut, and his cattle may all be swept away and very probably drowned. On the other hand, if the monsoon rains are too weak, there will be a drought again before the crops have had time to grow. Any of

A bullock pulling a car out of a flooded river

these disasters bring famine, and the peasant and his family starve.

In some places during the monsoon period it rains most of the time; in other places it rains for a few hours every day; in others, for a few days each week. There are a few places, for example, in part of north India and Pakistan, where even in the monsoon season it rains very little, and there are deserts.

Before the monsoon 'breaks', the weather is very hot indeed, so hot that it hurts to walk bare-foot, as many Indians do, because the ground burns the soles of one's feet. Then huge grey and white clouds full of rain move across the land from the sea, and as they meet the hot air over the land, thunderstorms break out. This is the start of the monsoon. Then down comes the rain—not gentle rain as in England, but deluges of rain with huge raindrops. As much rain will fall in a few hours as falls over London in several months. Streets turn into rivers; rivers into torrents. Monkeys and other animals disappear from sight, seeking shelter where they can. In Britain, where people say it is always raining, less than 100 inches of rain fall in a year. There is a town called Cherrapunji in north-east India, which is said to have more rain than anywhere else in the world, and this has between 600 and 900 inches a year—and it all falls in less than 4 months.

The monsoon rains in these countries make it possible to live; but also they make great difficulties. It is necessary, for example, to build very strong roads, for anything else would be washed away. Also, since plains and low-lying lands may become flooded for 3 months or more every year, roads and railways have to be made along embankments, lifted above the floods. Bridges are a very serious problem. For perhaps 9 months of the year, a river may be quite small, needing only a small bridge to cross it. Then comes the monsoon, and the river very quickly becomes several times as wide, so that only a very long bridge is of any use. Long bridges are expensive to build, so, except where a railway line has to cross a river, ferries are often used instead of bridges for carrying cars, carts, people, and animals. It is good fun crossing a river by ferry, but it is very slow. During the dry season, when the wide river bed has only a narrow stream running down it, people cross by fords. But it is difficult to tell how deep the water is, and cars often get stuck in the middle and have to be pulled out by bullocks.

People living in monsoon countries such as India and Burma, where they are so dependent on the weather, usually pray to and make offerings to the gods whom they believe control the monsoon.

19 Wild Life of the Jungle

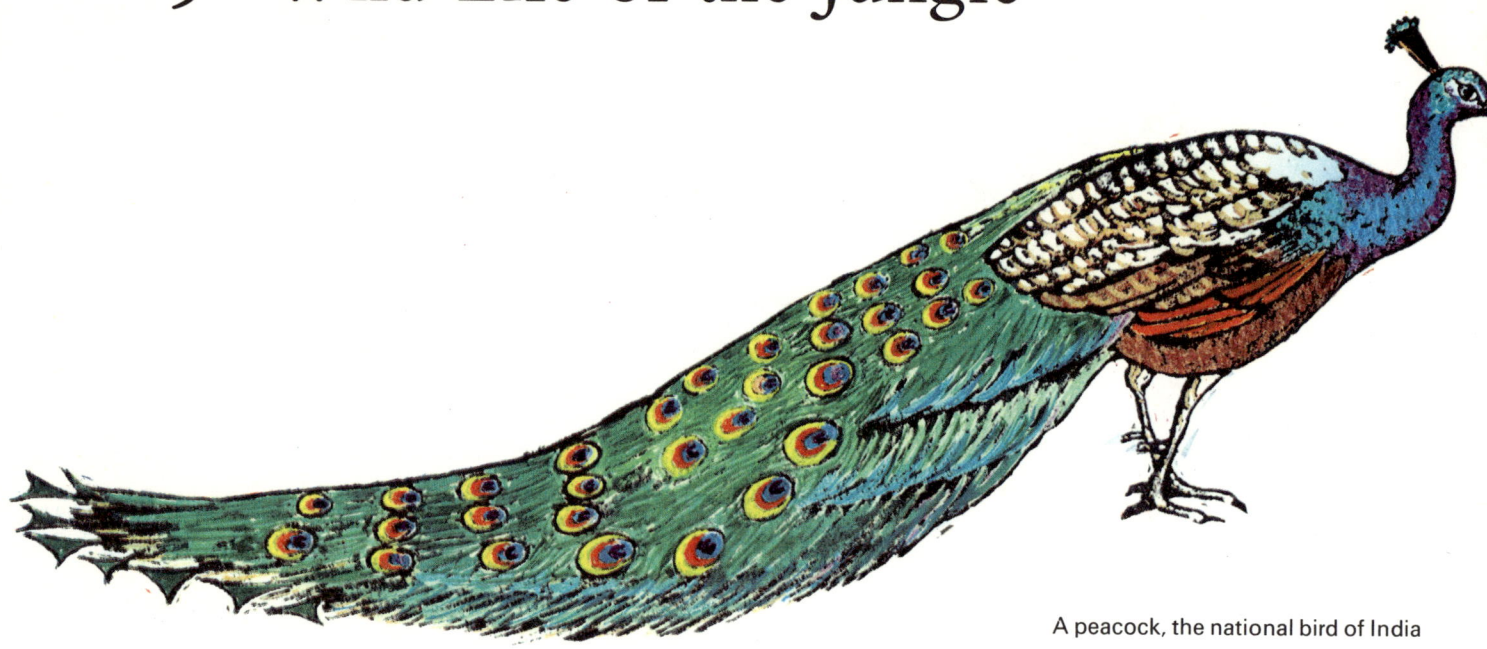

A peacock, the national bird of India

INDIA IS THE land of tigers and poisonous, hooded snakes called cobras. King cobras are sometimes as long as 16 feet, but the common cobra is not more than 5 feet long. There are also many leopards and tigers, and in some places huge one-horned rhinoceroses; and there are crocodiles in the rivers. Jackals and hyaenas are scavengers, and the repulsive-looking black vultures descend in hundreds on any dead animal. India is the home of the Indian elephants, which are usually not dangerous at all, though they do much damage by eating trees and trampling crops. There are many kinds of deer and wild cattle and also monkeys.

The many beautiful birds vary from tiny vivid creatures no bigger than butterflies to the giant cranes, which always go about in pairs and are as tall as a man. Wherever there are water buffaloes, there are lovely little white egrets which stand on their backs and pick grubs off their skins. Wild peacocks and brilliantly-coloured pheasants and jungle fowl live in the jungle and make a great deal of noise.

In many parts of India big game sanctuaries have been made where no one may kill a wild animal. In some of these it is possible for people to go and see the animals and watch how they live. There is a fine game sanctuary in Assam in north-east India, where the jungle is thick, and the bamboo grass is called elephant grass because it is so tall that wild elephants can hide in it. When people visit it, they ride on elephants.

Riding on an elephant is rather like being on a ship, for an elephant sways from side to side as it walks. A platform is fixed on the elephant's back, on which four or six people

A king Cobra

can sit, and the driver, or mahout, sits on its neck. The elephant moves steadily through the dense, long grass. If a rhinoceros is about, the elephant treads gently so as not to disturb or frighten it, for rhinoceroses are so stupid that if they are alarmed they will charge wildly, even though there is no danger.

An expedition into the game sanctuary may take most of a day and night. During the day one may see deer and probably bison, and perhaps several families of wild pigs running through the grass in single file, the boar in front, then the piglets, and the sow at the end. If one is lucky, there may be wild elephants bathing in the river, and perhaps one can see a cow elephant spraying her calf with water from her trunk.

At night one may be able to watch tigers and leopards come down to a water hole, and hear the uncanny laughing cry of jackals and possibly the howls of hyaenas echoing through the jungle. A snake may be hanging from a tree overhead, but unless it is touched, it probably will not attack. Most wild animals do not attack human beings except in self-defence, though sometimes old tigers and leopards who are no longer quick enough to overtake deer, become man-eaters because they are hungry. Anyone who is out at night in Assam, as in many parts of India, must protect himself from mosquitoes and sleep under a mosquito net, even in the house. The Assam mosquitoes carry the disease malaria, which is a serious disease in hot countries.

A Bengal tiger

20 Village Life in India: 1

ALTHOUGH THERE ARE big cities in India, far the greater number of people still live in villages. India is a country of villages, so if you want to see how the ordinary Indian family lives you must visit a village. Naturally life in the villages differs according to where the village is; but there is very much which is the same in almost all villages. We are going to follow a day in the lives of Ram and Sita and their children, Hari aged 11, Lila aged 7, and the baby Babu. In their part of India millet is the main crop. In other parts the main crop might be rice or wheat or tea or jute or coconuts; but life in the village would not be so different.

Ram gets up in the morning with the sun and goes out to the pond to have a dip. He cleans his teeth by chewing a twig and has a wash by the well. While he eats his breakfast, his wife Sita fans the flies away; and then he ties on his turban to protect his head from the hot sun and sets off to work. He harnesses his pair of bullocks and carries on his shoulder the wooden plough he made out of the branch of a tree, and he goes to his little fields to plough. After he has finished ploughing, he has a little rest in the shade of a tree, and then spends an hour or so with his bullocks, drawing water from the well to irrigate his land. Today is not a busy day because he does not have to take the potter's

Children in school

pots to the market in his wooden cart. So, his work over, he walks slowly back to the village, talking to his bullocks as he goes.

He joins his friends who are squatting in the shade under a big mango tree in the centre of the village and takes his turn at the hubble bubble pipe. While they inhale the smoke of tobacco, they all discuss the weather, the crops, and the news that a few miles away a new high school is going to be built. Ram says that if his eldest son Hari does well in the village school he will send him on to the new school. The school will be 1½ hours' walk away, but that is no matter, for Hari is sturdy. Already Hari has been helping his father by reading things out for him, for Ram never went to school; there was no school when he was a boy. Some of the others say Ram had much better put Hari to work, but Ram wants Hari to have better chances than he had.

While Ram is in his fields, Hari goes to school, barefoot and wearing khaki shorts and a white shirt. He is lucky that the school is in his village, for some children have to walk as much as 5 miles from other villages. The school consists of one room with one teacher and a large blackboard. Hari sits with the other boys cross-legged on the floor with his slate. There are no books, so the children learn to read from the board and copy on to their slates. They learn a great deal by heart. There are some girls in the school, but most are boys.

This afternoon there is a meeting of the village council in the school. The village council has decided to help the government to build the new school, and the villagers will be asked to help with their labour and with money. Ram is quite willing to work, but he has no money to spare. In fact, he hardly has any money at all, except what the potter pays him to take his pots to market.

He uses money very little, for he grows everything he needs to feed his family—the millet, the onions, the sugar, and the spices. All he ever buys with money is salt, matches, kerosene, and occasionally a piece of soap. Other things he needs, such as coarse village-made cloth for the family's clothes, he pays for with some of his crops—so many onions for a length of cloth, for example. If the crops are poor, as they have been this year, Ram does not buy cloth, and everybody eats a bit less.

After the village council, Ram goes for his weekly visit to the travelling barber, who is in the village today. Ram has a shave, a hair cut, and a nail cut. He does not do these things for himself, for he has neither razor nor scissors; in any case it is the tradition to go to the barber, and at the end of each month Ram gives the barber a pound of millet and an onion as payment.

When it is dark, Ram goes back to his hut, leaves his heavy leather sandals at the door, and is ready for dinner, already steaming in the pots. This consists mainly of millet with chopped-up onions and other vegetables, made tasty with spices. Ram can never eat all he would like; otherwise there would be none left for the family, who do not eat until he has finished. They all go to sleep early, sleeping in their clothes on straw mats on the ground. As he takes off his turban before lying down, Ram knows that Sita has fed the bullocks and that all is well, but he reminds himself that tomorrow he must start mending the thatch on the roof to keep out the rain when the monsoon rains start in a few days' time.

Ploughing with bullocks

21 Village Life in India: 2

SITA STARTS HER day, just as Ram does, by taking a bath in the village pond. She bathes in her cotton sari, which soon dries in the hot Indian sun. She dips her long black hair in the water and scrubs herself with pumice stone: soap is much too expensive to use except for special occasions. She coils her wet hair up into a bun and sticks a flower into it. Then she goes back to her hut to prepare breakfast.

Ram and Sita's hut has only two rooms, and it is made of dried mud pasted over a framework of bamboo sticks, with a thatched roof. The floor is made of beaten earth;

Sita grinding millet between two round stones

there is hardly any furniture, and the only lighting is from a kerosene lamp, which they use as little as possible because kerosene oil is expensive. They go to bed when it is dark and get up when it is light. There is a little back-yard with a small shed where Sita does her cooking.

Before she starts work Sita says a little prayer to the family god, who sits in a niche near the kitchen shed. Then she lights the fire to heat the clay oven. Wood and coal are difficult to get, and Sita uses instead cow-dung mixed with chopped straw and shaped into flat blocks, which are dried hard in the sun. It is Lila's job to make these. When the fire is started, Sita calls Lila to come and fan it. The cow-dung fuel gives off a lot of smoke which makes Lila's eyes smart.

Breakfast consists of the leftovers from the day before—a few pancakes of coarsely-ground millet flour, a pickled onion, and red-hot chilli sauce. Sita puts this on a brass tray and carries it to Ram, who sits cross-legged on the floor and eats with his fingers. When Ram has finished and gone off to work, Hari, Lila, and baby Babu have their breakfast. They get a pancake each, a little bit of pickled onion and sauce, and a small lump of coarse sugar.

After breakfast Hari goes off to school. Lila, who is now 7 years old, would like to go too; several of her friends do. But while Babu is a baby she must look after him. Sometimes she can put him to sleep in a hammock, but most of the time she carries him with her, astride her hip. Even when she goes outside the village to mind the family goat, she still carries Babu on her hip, not daring to put him down in the shade of a tree for fear of snakes or scorpions.

While Lila is busy making cow-dung cakes, Sita sweeps through the hut with her home-made broom of twigs, and cleans the floor and walls with cow-dung mixed with water, which helps to keep the flies and ants away and makes a clean fresh smell. Then she starts to prepare the day's food. She goes to her heavy grinding mill, made of two slabs of stone and a rough wooden handle, and grinds the millet between the stones ready for to-day's pancakes. Then she fetches water from the village well, which she carries in three brass jars balanced on her head. She calls Lila to come and knead the millet flour, mixed with water and salt, into little balls ready to be flattened out and baked, and also to clean the millet ready for tomorrow. Lila squats on the ground in front of the hut and picks out all the little stones and other rubbish.

Then Sita and Lila go up to the vegetable patch to pick the green chillis, which they spread out in the sun to dry before the rain rots them. After this, Lila takes a jar of tea and a pancake to Ram in the fields; and then she is able to go and play with her friends for a little. They play with pebbles, each trying to see how many pebbles they can throw up and catch again with one hand. But soon Lila sees her father bringing the bullocks in, and she must go and take them to the pond to scrub them with straw, and then feed them with chopped straw and bits of coarse sugar.

Often Sita has to help Ram in the fields, but just now there is no harvesting or planting to be done. So when she has cooked the supper and everyone is fed, she cleans the brass trays with ashes and mud, gives a little offering of coarse sugar to the family god, and lays out the straw mats on which all the family are soon sound asleep.

Lila and Babu

22 Sanganeer, a Rajasthan Village

SANGANEER IS A village like many others in Rajasthan in north-west India. It is beautiful and very clean. The streets are wide and swept clean by the village sweepers. The houses are made of dried mud, with small windows to keep out the heat. They have flat roofs on which the women sit during part of the day and also dry their vegetables and their clothes. The houses of Sanganeer are made gay by the bright paintings which decorate the walls. For instance, one house has on the front of the porch an aircraft diving into a fully-armoured elephant, on which rides a hero wearing a turban and armed with an old-fashioned sword. On another house is a small steam train puffing its white smoke over a sleepy tiger, who is chewing a red flower; and on another is painted a flock of peacocks, bright green and blue. The peacock is the sacred bird of Rajasthan; the country swarms with wild peacocks which are so tame that they not only steal the crops but food from the houses. Both they and the monkeys, which are also sacred, know that nobody will harm them and so they can do as they like.

The houses in Sanganeer are larger than in most Indian villages, and whole families live in one house—the father and mother, the sons and their wives and children, and other relations. The houses are built around a courtyard surrounded by mud walls. The richer houses have their own private well in the courtyard so that the women do not have to go outside to draw water from the village well. The better-off people like to keep their women in purdah, as Muslims do, so they do not go outside their own courtyard.

The women wear wide gathered skirts which sweep the ground, and pretty embroidered blouses. They cover their heads and faces with flimsy, brightly printed shawls. The men have huge moustaches; their colourful turbans flow in the breeze; and their embroidered leather slippers have turned-up toes. Both men and women wear earrings, and the women wear many other jewels. A well-to-do peasant's wife wears, besides her earrings, a nose ring, toe rings, rings on her fingers, a silver belt, armlets, anklets, silver buttons on her blouse, and a necklace. If she is rich, the jewels are of gold or silver; if she is poor they are made of tin. Only if she is a widow will she wear no jewels. In India a family does not put its savings into a bank, as we would do, but instead they buy jewels. When money is needed to buy a bullock or pay for a funeral, the jewels are sold. The jewellers of Rajasthan are well-known throughout India, both for their silver work and enamel work

Men betting on the weather

A woman printing cloth in the courtyard of her house

which they learnt from the Muslims. In Sanganeer there is a jewellers' street in which the silversmiths can be seen at work, hammering away on their small anvils.

Rajasthan villages are famous for their cotton-printing. The women sit on their roofs and in their courtyards dyeing and printing the pieces of cloth which they make into skirts, saris, or turbans to be sold all over India. They use hand-carved wooden blocks for printing traditional designs on the cloth. Except for looking after the printing blocks, which is the men's work, all the work is done by the women, while the men are busy in their fields growing cotton, castor-oil seeds, millets, and wheat. Bullocks pull the ploughs, and camels are used for turning the water wheels and pulling the carts laden with crops to the market. Camels are very suitable for working in a country like Rajasthan where it rains very little and water is precious, for they can go a long time without drinking.

One of the favourite pastimes of the men in Sanganeer is betting on whether it will rain or not. It only rains in Rajasthan for a short while during the monsoon season, which lasts from June to October. Some people who are good at telling when and where it will rain take bets with peasants that it will rain on some particular field in, say, 3 days. The farmer is glad to know, for if it is going to rain he need not irrigate his field. If the rain expert is right, the farmer pays him money; if he is wrong he pays the farmer a fine. Rain experts are so good that they usually make enough money to live on by betting on rain. Sometimes the villagers bet on how the clouds in the sky will move, just as people in England bet which horse will win a race. They will bet on which cloud will cross the horizon first, or which will first burst into rain. The villagers get quite as excited as we do over horse-racing, and they call out to their favourite cloud, urging it to hurry on so that they will win.

23 Gangatia, a Bengal Village

GANGATIA IS A village in Bengal in eastern India. Bengal has much more rain than many parts of India, and everywhere is green with trees and grass. There is plenty of water for growing crops, and so the people are not so poor as in other parts; though there are sometimes terrible floods which destroy the crops.

Gangatia has no road, but a footpath runs to the next village, lined with tall banyan trees with green creepers hanging from them. There are big bamboo clumps in which tigers and snakes may hide, and also tall coconut trees laden with clusters of coconuts, with monkeys jumping from tree to tree. Nobody lives very far away from a river.

Instead of living in one house, a Gangatia family has a little group of small huts made of bamboo matting and thatched with coconut leaves—a cook house, a sleeping house, a tool house, and a house for the animals. The huts are built round a pool which looks emerald green because of the weeds which grow at the bottom. The family get all their water for washing, cooking, and drinking from their own pool. They have to clear the pond out every day to prevent its getting choked by water hyacinth. About 100 years ago an English lady brought a water hyacinth plant in a pot and planted it in her garden because she loved its beautiful pale mauve flower. It grew so well that now it is a terrible weed, choking rivers and ponds.

Apu and his sister Durga live with their father and mother in Gangatia. Their father is the village potter, so he does not grow rice and jute crops as the other villagers do. He makes pots, and people pay him for their pots by giving him rice and coconuts and vegetables. Apu, who is 9, goes to school, but there are so many jobs for Durga to do at home that there is no time for school.

A statue of the goddess Durga at the time of her festival

The first thing Durga does in the morning is to put out a little dish of milk for the cobra who lives in the tool house. Snakes, like monkeys, are sacred to the people of Bengal, and so, although there are many snakes, and some of them, like cobras, are poisonous, they are never killed. Then Durga cleans out the pond and has her morning bath, while her mother feeds and milks the water buffalo. After that they prepare the day's meal—boiled rice flavoured with grated coconut, curdled buffalo's milk, pickled tomatoes, and a little bit of fish caught from the river and fried in mustard oil.

Durga is called after the goddess Durga, the patron goddess of Bengal. Every year in October comes the festival of the goddess Durga, and everyone is busy for days before making preparations for it, not only in Gangatia but in all the villages. They all compete with each other to make the best festival procession. According to the legend, the goddess Durga kills with one stroke of the sword the demon of evil who has hidden inside a young buffalo. The children's father, being the potter, makes a statue of the goddess in sun-dried mud, and the women dress it in a gaily-coloured sari and decorate it with tinsel and paint. Then they mount the statue of Durga and also of the demon wearing a buffalo's head on a decorated bullock cart and drive them in a slow procession through the paddy (rice) fields towards the river. All the people make merry and beat drums and cymbals to drive away any snakes or tigers that may be about. When, chanting and singing, the procession reaches the river, the goddess and demon are thrown into the water. Everyone throws garlands of flowers after them, and the statues sink into the water and disappear.

Then all the people return singing to their village for a feast. A goat, or a young buffalo shared between several villages, is killed, and everyone feasts on meat curry and sweetmeats which the women have been making for days before. Cows and bullocks are sacred to Hindus and may not be eaten, but water buffaloes are not; so the young buffalo can be killed and eaten by everyone.

Apu and Durga's father making pots on a potter's wheel which he pushes round with a stick

24 Nayagaon, a Village in the Punjab

THE PUNJAB IN the north is very different from the rest of India. The people are taller and sturdier, perhaps because they have better food and because the climate is more healthy—cold in winter and dry and hot in summer. There is very little rain in the Punjab, so farmers have to irrigate their crops. The water for irrigation comes either from wells or from canals which have been built to carry the water from the big rivers all over the country. Today the water from wells is usually pumped by small electric or diesel engines, though there are still some old-fashioned wells with water-wheels worked by bullocks. Farmers in the Punjab sometimes own a tractor or a truck instead of only bullock carts; and there are good roads over most of the country.

The Punjabi farmers not only grow food for themselves and their animals but also crops for sale—we call these 'cash crops' because they are sold in the market for cash. This means the farmer has some money which he can spend on things he cannot grow and some to save against bad times. It is quite common in the Punjab for houses to have small safes where the farmer can keep his money or valuable jewels. Wheat is the most important crop, but the farmers also grow maize, sugar-cane, groundnuts, and some cotton. The groundnuts (or peanuts) are crushed to produce oil for cooking.

Manu Tandon is a farmer living in Nayagaon, which means 'new village'. He lives in a house made of bricks of baked mud, with a flat roof, and built round a courtyard in which much of the family's daily activities are carried on. Inside the house, there is some furniture: for example, everybody sleeps on a string cot, instead of on the floor as they do in southern India. Manu is quite well off because he not only sells the cotton and groundnuts which he grows but he also owns a tractor, the only tractor in the village, and he makes money hiring his tractor to his neighbours. Manu's brother, who lives with him, owns a truck and earns money carrying goods all over the Punjab. Also Maya, Manu's wife, has a sewing machine, and when she has finished her household work, she squats in a corner of the courtyard with her sewing machine and makes uniforms, which she sells to the high school in Nayagaon. So altogether quite a lot of money comes in to the family.

Manu is not the only prosperous person in Nayagaon; his neighbour, Tara Singh, runs a small bicycle factory in an old cattle shed. Tara Singh's young nephew Hira paints the mudguards of the bicycles with bright colours, never forgetting to put on the front a brightly-coloured butterfly so that everybody can recognize a Tara Singh bicycle. The boys and girls often come to the high school from far-away villages riding Tara Singh bicycles. Everybody in the Punjab wears trousers, girls as well as boys, which is convenient when riding a bicycle.

Manu and his tractor are in great demand whenever there is a wedding in Nayagaon. The bridegroom used to come to fetch his bride riding a white mare, as was the custom all over India. He used to ride to the home of his bride dressed in brocade with a flowing turban, on a white mare bedecked with floral garlands and tinsel. Musicians walked in front and behind him. Now it is considered more modern and smarter for the bridegroom to arrive on a tractor, which is also decorated with garlands and tinsel, and after the wedding to take his bride back to his home on the tractor. The marriage ceremonies, which have not altered much, last for 3 or 4 days, and all the friends and the relatives

Punjabi men dancing. They jump high with joy and shout

come to witness the ceremony and to eat and sing and dance. The priest lights a sacred fire, and the bride and bridegroom, tied together by a knot in their clothes, have to walk seven times round the fire, making vows. When they have done this they are husband and wife, and they go off on the tractor to the groom's home.

The great festival in Nayagaon and most of northern India, held in February, is Holi. Holi does not celebrate anything in particular, but it is a general holiday, when everyone makes merry and children have a great deal of fun. The custom is to squirt coloured water at everybody else. The children at the Holi festival can be as impertinent as they like and squirt coloured water even at the most respected of elders. Nobody wears his best clothes for Holi; people throw crackers, let off lovely fireworks, and play drums and cymbals, and many people get very excited and rowdy.

25 The River Ganges

THE GANGES, INDIA'S great sacred river, is 1500 miles long from its source in the Himalayan mountains to the sea. It is seven times as long as the river Thames. After it has come down from the mountains, it flows through a fertile plain across north India. The Ganges plain is as big as Britain, and about three times as many people live there as in Britain. During the heavy rains and cloud bursts of the monsoon, so much water comes down the river that it spreads over the plains like a great lake; in some places the river becomes 7 to 10 miles wide. Even during the dry season the Ganges is between 2 and 3 miles wide in some places, so wide that one cannot see one bank from the other.

As the Ganges and its tributaries flow down from the mountains, they bring with them very fertile mud, called silt. Each time the river floods it carries this silt with it and drops it on the fields, making a very rich top soil on which sugar-cane, rice, jute, and other crops grow well. The soil is so rich that people on the Ganges plain can grow three crops in one year.

The people who live along the Ganges speak different languages, live in different ways, and grow different crops. Up in the hills the people live in stone houses and grow fruit trees and corn, and keep sheep. Down in the plain they grow wheat, sugar-cane, and cotton and keep cattle, and they live in houses made out of mud bricks. Farther down the river, past the sacred city of Benares, the people grow rice and jute; and in Bengal (see Chapter 23) they live in houses built of bamboo with thatched roofs. As the Ganges flows near to the sea it breaks into the many branches of its delta, and the northern branches flow through East Pakistan. The people in this part of Pakistan live in just the same way as the people in

West Bengal, speak the same language, and grow much the same crops (see Chapter 34).

All Hindus believe that the Ganges is a sacred river, and that when a good Hindu dies, his ashes should be taken to the Ganges and scattered in the river. They have a legend that thousands of years ago there was a lovely maiden called Ganga who lived high up in the mountains with her father, King Himalaya, after whom the mountains were called. In the plain below lived a very proud king who had 60,001 sons. This king thought himself as great as the gods, and the god Vishnu punished him by burning all his sons to ashes, except one. Vishnu told the arrogant king that unless the ashes of the 60,000 sons were washed in the tears of the beautiful maiden Ganga, their souls would not go to heaven. The king did everything he could to persuade Ganga to come down to the plain, but she would not. After he died, his one remaining son, who became king, also failed to persuade Ganga. But his son, Bhagiratha, was so good and pious a king and prayed so humbly to the gods that the god Shiva took pity on him. He turned the maiden Ganga into a river flowing out of his own head in a terrific torrent, which dashed down the mountains and through the plain, washing the ashes of the 60,000 princes to heaven. The river Ganges still goes on washing the ashes of all good Hindu people to heaven.

All the big cities on the banks of the Ganges are sacred cities to which Hindus make pilgrimages. Most important is Benares, to which hundreds of thousands of Hindus come every year to pray in the temples and bathe in the river to wash away their sins. They fill bottles with the holy water to take home with them. Some of the cities, such as Kanpur (Cawnpore) and Calcutta, are big industrial towns with many factories for manufacturing such things as sugar and cotton cloth.

The Ganges is a great waterway through north India. It is possible for boats to travel from the big cities higher up, down to Calcutta; and Calcutta, which stands on a branch of the Ganges called the Hooghly about 80 miles from the sea, is a large port to which ocean-going steamers come. All along the river big sailing-boats with large square sails pull huge bamboo rafts loaded high with raw material for the factories—jute, sugar-cane, rice, cotton, and other things.

The river is so wide that building bridges is very expensive, and in most places people cross the river by ferry boat or ford. There is a fine modern bridge below Patna, the ancient capital of King Ashoka in the state of Bihar (see Chapter 7). This bridge is over $2\frac{1}{2}$ miles long and carries a road and a railway. There is another huge modern bridge, called the Howrah Bridge at Calcutta, and there are bridges in the other big towns. But most of the millions of people who live all along the great Ganges plain live in villages one or other side of the mighty river and, if they have to cross at all, do so by sailing boats and rafts.

26 Chotagaon, a Village in the Deccan

THE DECCAN IS a rocky tableland in southern India, with a range of mountains running down the west side. Many rivers rise in the mountains and run eastwards, across the Deccan, down to the plains, and into the Bay of Bengal. During the heavy monsoon rains (see Chapter 18) from June to October, these rivers are like raging torrents; but through the winter and spring, when no rain falls at all, the rivers gradually dry up altogether, except for a few pools here and there. The country gets drier and drier, and the only water comes from wells which are cut deep down into the rock. In all the villages in the Deccan everyone is always thinking about water; and when at last the monsoon rains come, the people are so glad they sing and dance and beat drums. If the monsoon is late, the people starve.

Chotagaon, which means 'little village', has several wells. Twice a day the women draw up water in a brass bucket on a long rope to fill their own copper or pottery jars. Then they pile these one on the top of another on their heads, and walk steadily home, never spilling a drop. Little girls learn to carry water pots on their heads almost as soon as they can walk. The farmers draw water for irrigating the crops with huge 'buckets' made of buffalo skins. A pair of bullocks draw the great leather bags of water, hour after hour, patiently up from the well to flow into the fields. Today, some of the wells are fitted with mechanical pumps, which bring up the water far more quickly and save hours of patient work with bullocks.

The houses in Chotagaon are made of mud and thatched. They have only two rooms

Bullocks dressed up for a festival

and no windows, only peepholes to let in a little light. There is no chimney, so the rooms are generally full of smoke from the open fire where the cooking is done. The only furniture, except for sleeping mats which are rolled up during the day, is large pottery jars in which is stored all the grain the family will use from one harvest to the next. The only decoration is a coloured picture of the favourite god, the elephant-headed Ganesh. Outside, the house is made to look gay by the pumpkin plants which climb over the thatch. Pumpkins are like large round orange vegetable marrows, with large green leaves and yellow flowers.

In Chotagaon the animals live with the people, but today some houses have a separate animal shed for the bullocks and goats, though newly-born calves and kids generally come inside with the family.

Farming on the Deccan is hard work, for the soil is not very rich, and hardly anything will grow without irrigation. Everyone grows millet and onions and vegetables to feed the family, and perhaps a little rice. Then sugar-cane is a good crop because the local sugar factory a few miles away will give a good price for it. But it needs constant watering from the time the little green cuttings are planted in wet ground to the time it has grown into a thick plantation high enough to hide tigers and leopards, which often lurk in it. Every farmer keeps some of his crop to take to the village sugar-maker to make the hard brown sugar called 'gur'. The sweet sap is crushed out of the canes and boiled for hours in a huge iron pan until it is like toffee. Then the syrup is poured into clay jars or holes in the ground to cool.

Most farmers grow some cotton which they take to the local cotton factory. But some they take to the village weaver who makes it into cloth for their own clothes. As well as the sugar-maker and weaver, there is the village potter and the carpenter, whose fathers and grandfathers were potters or carpenters before them. But now that nearly all the boys and some of the girls go to school, some of them will no longer follow their fathers' trades but will become teachers or go to work in the cities.

The holidays in Chotagaon are the festivals. There is the festival of the bulls when everyone dresses up his bullocks with garlands and tassels and bells, and paints their horns in bright colours, and leads them in a procession through the village with music and singing. This brings good luck to the village.

The biggest festival is the festival of Ganesh in August. Ganesh, according to the Hindu legend, is the son of the god Shiva. He was born when Shiva was away on a long journey. When Shiva returned he was jealous to find a handsome young man in his house, and before his wife could tell him who the young man was, he cut off his head with his mighty sword. To make up for his terrible deed, he promised his wife to give Ganesh the head of the first creature to pass by. Then an elephant came by, and to punish Shiva for his jealousy, his only son goes through life with an elephant's head. Every year clay statues of Ganesh are made and carried in procession with singing and drums to be thrown into the river to bring luck to the village.

A woman of the Deccan carrying a pot of water on her head

59

27 Nade, a Village in Kerala

KERALA IS A LONG STRIP of flat land in south-west India, lying between a range of mountains and the sea. The clouds blow in from the sea and break into warm rain before they reach the mountains, so there are only 2 or 3 months in the year when there is no rain in Kerala. With so much warmth and wet, trees and crops grow well. There are tall, slender, feathery coconut trees everywhere, right down to the water's edge; there are paddy fields growing rice, and plantations of pepper, tea, bananas, pineapples, and nut trees. As no one lives very far from either the sea or rivers and lakes, there are always fish to be caught. In the forests inland there are monkeys, wild elephants, bison, wild pigs, and many other animals.

Picking coconuts

But although good crops can be grown, the people of Kerala are mostly very poor, and this is because there are many too many of them. There are about 1,130 people to the square mile, more than in any other state in India. Though most people are farmers, they only have very tiny farms, and have to do other work as well to make enough money to live on.

Achan and his wife Amma live in the village of Nade. Like most of the people in Kerala, they are slenderly built and have dark skins and black hair. As it is so warm, they need little clothing. The men wear a length of white cotton cloth wrapped round the waist, which they tuck up at the waist when they are working. The women wear saris, like other Indian women—sometimes white, sometimes brightly coloured. The little boys nowadays generally wear white shorts and a shirt.

Achan has a tiny plot of land on which he grows five coconut trees. He cuts off the coconuts with a sharp knife by climbing up the tress and throwing them down to Kuta, his eldest son. Then he sells them to the local factory. Only on special occasions do they keep any to eat themselves. The coir, which is the coarse fibrous covering of the nut, is used for making coconut matting, fishing nets, ropes, brushes, brooms, and carpets. The shells are used as fuel and also as cups and dippers. The flesh is good to eat and is nourishing because it has so much oil in it. In the factory it is crushed to extract the oil, which is used for cooking, for making things like soap and margarine, and for burning in lamps. Achan uses the dried coconut palm leaves for thatching his cottage.

Achan works as a 'coolie', a hired labourer, collecting the coconut coir in his hand-cart and taking it to the factory. Amma works in a cashew-nut factory, where she peels the cashew nuts ready for packing into tins to be sent abroad. When she has finished her work she walks back to her neat little house built of red stones and mud and prepares the family meal. This consists of a pot of rice, one or two baked bananas, and boiled roots of tapioca flavoured with very spicy chutney. Also there is often some fish, and the children sometimes have a piece of village-made sugar to chew.

Achan and Amma have eight children to feed, so they have to work hard. Achan himself went to school, and he is sending his children to school too. Kuta, who is 14, goes to the Mission school where he learns his lessons in English. He hopes to pass his matric examination, and then to go as a clerk to one of the big cities—Delhi, Bombay, or Calcutta. Then perhaps he will be able to send some money home to help his brothers and sisters. Kuti, the eldest girl, goes to the government school, where she is taught, not in English, but in Malayalam, the language of Kerala. Every morning in Nade a stream of children walk to school along the roadside, the boys on one side and the girls on the other. The schools are not in the village but in a place mid-way between several villages so that no one has too far to walk. More children go to school in Kerala than in most parts of India.

After school, it is Kuti's job to look after the pepper creepers and to collect the peppercorns ready for the man who comes round to buy them. Then she has to bathe her little brothers and sisters and take the family wash to the river. When she washes her own hair she rubs it with coconut oil to make it shiny. She has to be careful where she walks with her bare feet because of the poisonous snakes. When people go out after dark in Kerala they carry blazing torches with them to drive the snakes away.

There are holidays in Nade as well as work, even for the poorest families. Every year comes Diwali, the Festival of Lights, when everyone celebrates the triumph of Good over Evil. At Diwali the people all pay honour to their tools: farmers to their ploughs and hoes; factory workers to their machines; soldiers to their guns; and children to their pencils and blackboards. Before Diwali, Achan brings back a dozen little clay lamps, which Amma fills with coconut oil and coarse cotton wicks. The children decorate the roof and windows of their house with the lamps, and when the moon rises, Achan lights them. All the houses in Nade and in Kerala and over most of India are lit up for Diwali with lamps shining like stars. In Nade the river also is lit up with little lamps, which float downstream, carrying their flickering flames to the sea.

Transplanting rice

28 Modern India

A steel plant. Molten steel is being poured from a giant 'ladle'

INDIANS ARE PROUD of the progress India has made since she became independent. Although she is still mainly a country of villages, and seven out of every ten people depend in one way or another on the land for a living, India now also has factories and big industries. The government is spending a great deal of money building new factories and making power stations for generating electricity for them. If India is to find work and food for her 450 million or more people, she must become an industrial as well as a farming country. Today, the cotton and jute grown on the farms is being made into cloth and hessian in India's own factories, instead of all being sent to Europe. And India is beginning to make her own railway engines, aeroplanes, cars, and agricultural machines, instead of buying them all from abroad.

The government wants all Indians, especially children, to know what is being done, and what opportunities there now are for children leaving school. In a country as big as India it is not very easy to make all the people feel they belong to one country. The people growing coconuts in Kerala or tea in Assam live a very different life from those growing wheat or millet in the north. They eat different food, speak a quite different language, and sometimes follow a different religion. So the government collects school parties, one or two pupils from each secondary school in a district, and takes them to visit some of the important new projects so that they can see with their own eyes what their country is doing.

Govind and Raja are two schoolboys of 12 years old who were chosen by their schools to go on one of these excursions, starting from Delhi. Both their fathers are farmers, but they want to be engineers, so this was a wonderful opportunity for them. The first place they went to visit was the Bhakra Dam, which is in the very north of India on one of the branches of the Indus river.

Engineers build dams across rivers to hold back the water for different reasons. One reason is to store the water in an artificial lake during the wet season so that it can be used to irrigate the fields during the dry season. The water held by the Bhakra Dam is carried by canals all over the dry lands of Rajasthan and the Punjab, where it rains very little. Another reason for making dams in mountain rivers is to use the power of the water to drive turbines and generate electricity; and the Bhakra Dam makes electricity for the new factories and cities of northern India. There are many other dams in different parts of India, especially in the hills west of the Deccan, where electricity is made for the factories of Bombay and in those north-west of Calcutta. Some dams are built to stop the rivers flooding during the wet season, as well as to provide water in the dry season.

Govind and Raja were much impressed by how beautiful the dam and its great lake were, and Govind took photographs with his little box camera. But both boys were most looking forward to the visits to factories. They visited two government factories, one making railway engines and the other railway carriages. Govind made up his mind immediately to be a railway engineer; but Raja was most excited by the great steel mill which they next visited. While Govind was taking photographs, Raja collected booklets and coloured pictures of blast furnaces and of molten steel being poured into tanks. He was certain that he would be a steel engineer.

Wherever the school party visited, they were made welcome, and someone took them round, explaining what was happening and answering their questions. The last visit was to a chemical works at a new town called Sindri. Here the government is making fertilizers to be sent all over India so that the village farmers can help to make their land grow better crops. Both boys looked forward to telling their fathers about this. The chemicals used in the fertilizers are stored in huge balloon-like domes which glisten like silver in the strong sun. The children also watched girls putting penicillin into little bottles called vials, ready to be sent to the hospitals and clinics throughout India.

As they sat in the train carrying them back to Delhi, all the children of the party felt they now understood better how their country was progressing, and they felt proud to be Indians. Now they would go back to their own schools, and tell the others what exciting things they had seen, and what modern India was like.

Building the Bhakra Dam

29 The Cities of India

The Red Fort, Delhi

A Calcutta policeman. Behind him is the Howrah Bridge

EACH OF THE different States of the Republic of India has a capital city, and some of them have about a million or more people in them. Some of the cities, such as Delhi, are old, but many have grown in the last 100 years, while some, where the government has built factories, are quite new. These new factory towns, making steel, or railway engines, or fertilizers, grow bigger as people leave the villages in which their families have lived for generations and seek work in the cities.

The capital of India is Delhi. Old Delhi was the capital of the Mogul Emperors (see Chapter 10). It was mostly built in the early 17th century of red sandstone, and had a great wall round it. It is crowded and picturesque with colourful bazaars selling ivory, gold, and silver work, jewellery, and embroidery. The streets are full of pilgrims and visitors from all over India, and cattle sit about in the streets and must not be disturbed because they are sacred. There is a splendid fortress called the Red Fort, and the largest mosque in India. Beyond the walls are the remains of an older city which was destroyed by the Muslim invaders.

The new city consists almost entirely of handsome government buildings, a palace where the Viceroy used to live, and modern villas for government officials. Delhi is not now as important for trade and industry as Bombay or Calcutta because it is not a port.

64

Calcutta, which was founded in 1690 by the East India Company (see Chapter 12), is a huge, overcrowded busy city, with a hot, damp climate. It is on a branch of the Ganges called the Hooghly, across which a great bridge is built to connect Calcutta with Howrah. The river is crowded with every kind of shipping from ocean steamers to picturesque local sailing boats and barges piled high with crops from the country. The centre of Calcutta has fine houses and public buildings, but the outskirts are overcrowded with insanitary, narrow streets where hundreds of thousands of people live in any kind of shack in great poverty.

Another very big Indian city is Bombay. The Indians call it their most modern city, and it is the most attractive to live in. In June, when the monsoon rains come, it is very wet indeed for a time; but during the rest of the year, though the sun is very hot, there are cooling sea breezes, for Bombay is built on an island on the west coast of India.

Today Bombay has over 4 million people, but it has not always been a big city. In 1661, when the island first became British, Bombay was no more than a village. The East India Company made a trading centre and a port there because of its very good natural harbour, and by the eighteenth century it had become the headquarters of the Company. During the nineteenth century it grew, partly because it was the most convenient port for ships coming from Europe, and partly because all the cotton grown in the rich lands of the Deccan was sent down to Bombay to be exported. Then spinning and weaving factories grew up in Bombay to make the Indian cotton into cloth. The port grew bigger and busier, and is now a more important port than Calcutta on the other side of India, for most of the imports and exports to and from Europe come through Bombay.

People coming to India from Britain by ship most probably come to Bombay. As the ship approaches, their first sight of India is the lovely harbour. When they land at the port, they come into a modern city with a promenade along the beach and elaborate nineteenth-century buildings, such as the Victoria Railway Terminus (rather like St. Pancras in London) and the University. There are many modern blocks of offices and business houses. In fact, the centre of Bombay would not look so different from a modern European city were it not for the hot sun and the people. There are people from all parts of India, mostly wearing white clothes, and there always seems to be a crowd.

New houses and new streets are being built all the time for the many people who are coming to Bombay to work in the factories, the port, or the big commercial houses. But there are still not nearly enough houses and, as in Calcutta, thousands of people live in miserable hovels built of bits of wood and old tin on the outskirts of the city. Many have no homes at all.

The Gateway of India. This archway stands near the entrance to Bombay harbour

30 The Republic of Pakistan

A tribesman and his wife from the north of Pakistan moving from the mountains to the plains for the winter

WHEN THE BRITISH left India (see Chapter 16), the people who were Muslims, followers of Mohammed, wanted to have a country of their own and to be ruled by a government which was Muslim. So those parts of northern India where the majority of the people were Muslims joined together to make a new country called Pakistan, which means 'land of the pure'.

Unfortunately the Muslim parts of India do not lie together, so Pakistan is a very peculiar country consisting of two parts—West Pakistan and East Pakistan—which are about 1,000 miles away from each other. The high Himalaya Mountains (see Chapter 36) run along the north and west of West Pakistan, and the river Indus (see Chapter 32) flows from the mountains to the Arabian sea. Were it not for the Indus, much of Pakistan would be almost a desert. On the west lie two other Muslim countries, Afghanistan and Persia (see Map p. 1). East Pakistan is quite different. It lies north-east of India with Burma on its eastern borders, and the big river Brahmaputra runs through it. It has plenty of water, and the soil is very fertile. Although it is much smaller than West Pakistan, more people live in it—more people than there is food to feed, and so they are poorer than the people of the west.

The people are as different from each other as the countries are. In fact, the only thing the two parts of Pakistan have in common is their religion—they are both followers of Mohammed. The people of East Pakistan are much more like the people of Bengal in India. They speak the same language, Bengali; they wear the same kind of clothes—the men, a long plain loin cloth called a dhoti,

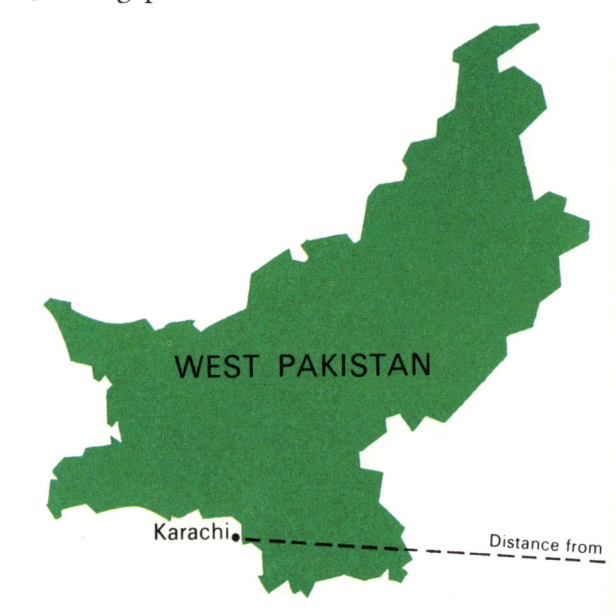

পাকিস্তান

The word 'Pakistan', written in Bengali. It is read from left to right. Bengali is spoken by the people of East Pakistan

پاکستان

The word 'Pakistan', written in Urdu which is the language spoken by the people of West Pakistan. It is read from right to left

and the women, a sari; they grow the same crops, and live mostly on rice (see Chapter 34). In West Pakistan most people speak a language called Urdu, and if the men do not wear European clothes, they wear trousers with often gaily embroidered waistcoats and turbans. The women are not free to go about as they are in East Pakistan, but have to wear tent-like robes called burkhas, which cover them from head to foot so that no man except their husbands may look at them.

West and East Pakistan, separated from each other by India

Karachi to Dacca about 1500 miles — EAST PAKISTAN • Dacca

The biggest town in Pakistan is Karachi, which is a port on the west coast and has some factories. Karachi is near the desert, and so there are camel carts in the streets as well as trucks and cars. It is very hot and dry, it hardly ever rains, and there are fearful dust storms; but in the evening there is a cool breeze from the sea, and people go out to walk along the sandy shore or go sailing.

The capital of West Pakistan is the ancient city of Lahore, which has an old University, beautiful gardens made by one of the Muslim Emperors in the seventeenth century, and one of the biggest mosques in the world. Dacca is the capital of East Pakistan. Everything in Dacca is green because of the warm damp climate, and the gardens have beautiful flowering trees and flowers such as orchids. In the jungle, which is not far away, there are snakes and tigers.

The capital of all Pakistan is a quite new city called Islamabad, which has been built specially as a capital. It is still not very large. There are a few other quite big towns, but Pakistan, like India, is a land of villages, and we can see best how the people live by visiting a village.

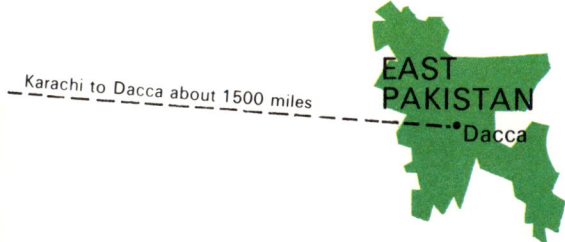

31 Pathans of the North-West Frontier

A Pathan father and son

THE PATHANS, WHO live in the rocky hills on the north-west of Pakistan, are tall and very handsome, with sharp noses, long beards, and light blue eyes. We cannot tell what the women look like for they always cover themselves when they leave their own part of the house. The Pathans live in fortified villages with towers and battlements round the high village walls. The houses are made of mud bricks plastered with mud. The men are always ready for a battle, and they love their guns even more than their women. One can often see a Pathan carrying two rifles as well as a couple of pistols and a couple of cartridge belts, just for the fun of it. Even little boys can be seen with real little rifles and guns and real cartridge belts. They make their own guns, and they are very good at copying the best models. They do this in their own houses by hand, without machines and often even without electricity.

The Pathans are very proud and quick to take an insult, so it can be dangerous for strangers to venture into their country unless they have a Pathan guide. The watchmen on the towers guarding the villages will shoot at strangers simply for the sake of shooting practice. On the other hand the Pathans, like many Muslim tribesmen, are most hospitable. A guest is sacred and must not be harmed. If anyone takes refuge in a Pathan village, the entire village may risk getting killed rather than surrender the refugee to the enemy.

The North-West Frontier Province is famous not only for its beautiful high passes over the mountains between India and Afghanistan, but also because so many battles have been fought there. This is the way the Muslim emperors from Afghanistan invaded India in the eleventh and twelfth centuries (see Chapter 9). When the British ruled

The bazaar in Peshawar

India, they were always having to send troops to subdue the Pathans and try to make them keep the peace. Even today, although the Pathans are very good farmers and excellent soldiers, they are not at all easy to govern, and battles will still break out between one family or village and another.

Between the high mountains there are sheltered valleys with very fertile soil, well watered by mountain streams. Here the Pathan farmers grow rice, tobacco, oranges, grape-fruits, sweet limes, grapes, and almonds. On the sheltered slopes they grow maize and wheat, and in the hills they keep flocks of fat-tailed sheep, called dumbas. These sheep store fat in their tails, as camels store fat in their humps. In the summer when there is good pasture, their tails grow very fat, and this helps them to get through the cold winter when food is scarce. If you were to visit a Pathan house as a guest, you would probably be given a delicious dish of mutton roasted on a spit in the open fire and eaten with a coarse but tasty pancake called *nan*, which the Pathans love.

There is much trade between Afghanistan and Pakistan across the North-West Frontier mountains, especially through the famous Khyber Pass which links the old city of Peshawar with Kabul, the capital city of Afghanistan. Today a motor road runs through the Khyber Pass, but there is still a steady stream of camel caravans. The camels are laden with dried fruit, salt, sheepskins, and carpets, and they make their slow and steady way through the wild and rocky country, always with a small donkey to lead them and bring good luck.

The caravans come to the gay and picturesque bazaar in the centre of Peshawar. Here, piled up in pyramids of bright colours and decorated with tinsel tassels, are dark-green water melons with crimson flesh, black and white grapes, oranges, grape-fruits and limes, mangoes and plums, maize cobs, tomatoes, dates, nuts, and many kinds of vegetables. As well as fruit, there are carpet and cloth sellers, stalls of sweetmeats, flowers, and various local crafts. The caravans and trucks carry back to Afghanistan cargoes of machinery and industrial goods.

32 The River Indus

THE RIVER INDUS, which flows from the Himalaya Mountains, right across Pakistan, into the Arabian Sea, is one of the great rivers of the world. It is 1,800 miles long, and is longer than any other river in the Indian continent. If it were not for the Indus and her tributaries, Pakistan would be a desert where no one could live. As it is, many millions of people both in West Pakistan and in northern India depend for their lives on the water which the Indus brings down from the mountains.

The Indus starts as melting ice from glaciers in the mountains just in Tibet (see Chapter 36). In the winter, when it is very cold, no ice and snow melt, and so only a trickle of water flows down the rivers. But in summer, when the sun is hot, the snow and ice melt very fast into thousands of little streams which flow into the river, and the Indus brings down vast quantities of water into Pakistan. This is just the opposite from the rivers of most countries, which bring down most water in the winter when it is raining in the mountains, and much less in the summer. A river which brings down so much more water at one time of year than at another raises problems. In the winter there is not enough water, and in the summer there is too much, and the river floods all over the plains of Pakistan. It is because of these floods that there are very few towns along the Indus, and the villages are usually 2 or 3 miles away from the river and are built wherever there is a hill.

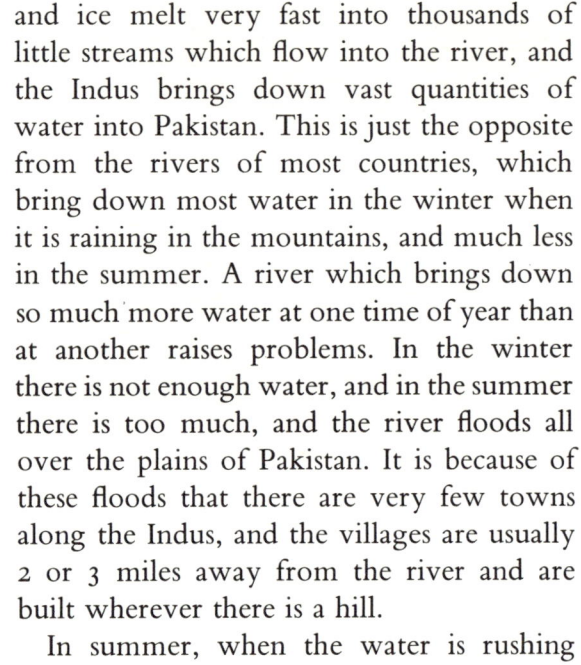

Cutting sugar-cane

In summer, when the water is rushing down the mountain streams and along the Indus and her tributaries, it brings with it a great deal of fertile silt, even more than the Ganges brings (see Chapter 25). When the water floods over the plains it drops this rich soil on to the land. When the water has drained off, the farmers of the Punjab (a word which means 'five rivers') can sow their crops of cotton and sugar-cane and wheat. In many parts the farmers can grow two crops of wheat in a season.

In old days a great part of the land through which the Indus flows was desert, growing nothing at all, and the cultivated land near the river was not easy to farm because of the floods. Also, when the river reached the very flat plains, the water flowed too slowly to carry all the amount of silt in it. So the silt sank on to the river bed and blocked it. Then, when the next wet season came round, the water would have to find a new course. Today engineers are finding ways of controlling the floods and also of storing all the surplus water of the four months of flood so that it can be used during the eight months of drought.

In 1932, when India and Pakistan were still being ruled by Britain, a great barrage across the Indus, near the town of Sukkur, was completed. This was called the Lloyd Barrage after Lord Lloyd, who was the Governor of that part of India. This barrage holds back the flood water and directs it into seven main canals. From these the water runs into smaller canals and then into still smaller ones, and is carried over 6,000 miles to irrigate more than 5 million acres of country which before this was too dry to grow crops at all.

This has been such a success that now there is a great plan to build very many more barrages and dams to control all the waters of the Indus and her five main tributaries, and also to make a whole network of canals all over the Punjab, both in Pakistan and India. The water is precious, and the people's lives depend on it, so the first thing which had to be decided was how the waters should be divided between Pakistan and India. In 1960 the two countries signed a treaty agreeing that Pakistan should have the waters of the Indus itself and of the two western tributaries, the Jhelum and the Chenab, and that India should have the waters of the three eastern rivers, the Ravi, the Beas, and the Sutlej.

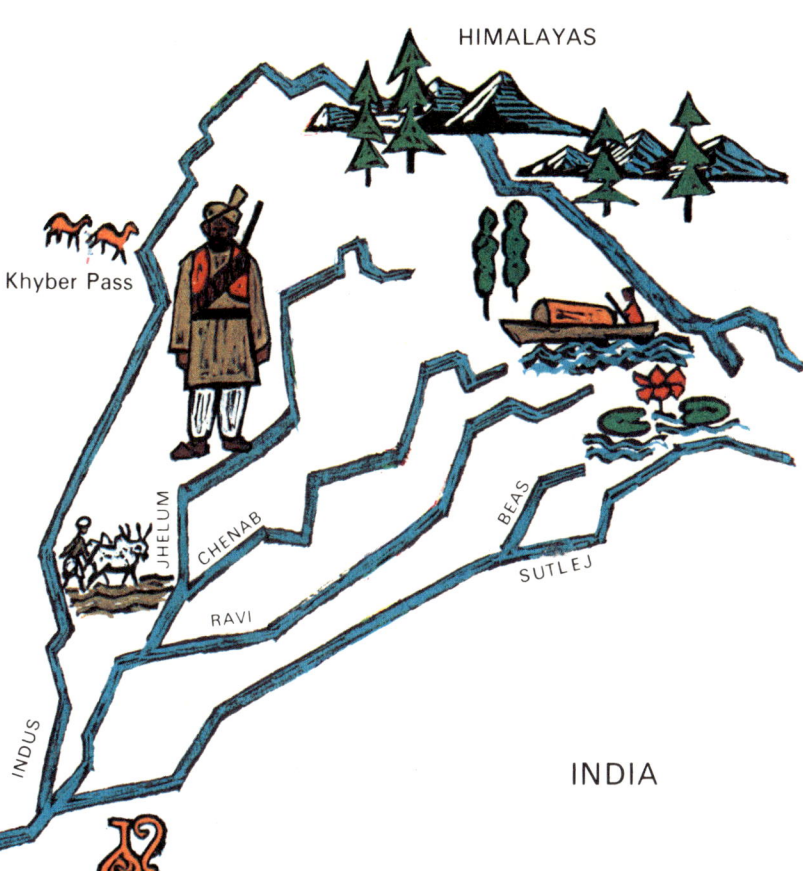

Many of the barrages and dams have now been built. Those built up in the mountains hold back the summer flood water in great artificial lakes and release it gradually through the dry season so that there is always water to run along the hundreds of miles of irrigation canals to the farmers' fields. Also big power stations are being built to make electricity for the towns and factories of West Pakistan and northern India.

When this great plan has been completed, the Indus will be the servant of the people of Pakistan and India, instead of being, as it often has been in the past, the master.

33 A Village in West Pakistan

PIR ALI IS A typical village in West Pakistan. Like most of West Pakistan, the country round Pir Ali would be a desert if water were not brought to it. Many villages depend almost entirely upon water brought from the mighty river Indus by irrigation canals, for it scarcely ever rains. But Pir Ali is better off than some villages for it can also get water from deep wells. In old days the water was brought up to the surface by great water wheels worked by the farmers' camels or bullocks. Today the water is pumped by little electric motors, for a few years ago a small electric generating station was built about 30 miles away, and this provides electricity for the whole district.

But most of the water comes to Pir Ali by canals. Water is necessary for life; nothing can be grown without it. But in a country where it does not rain and the sun is very hot, trouble can come when the fields are covered with irrigation water. The hot sun beating on the fields makes the water evaporate—that is, it draws much of the water up into the air as water vapour. This makes the soil begin to sweat, just as a person can sweat in very hot, damp weather. The sweating draws up salt from deep down in the ground and leaves it as a crust on the top of the soil, and the farmers' crops will not grow on land covered with salt. Somehow the salt has to be removed. The Pakistan Government has been busy finding ways of clearing off the salt. They find the best way is to pump up water from the wells and spray it over the fields to wash off the salt. Then they run the salty water into special drainage ditches, which carry it into big drainage canals to be taken away to the sea. All round Pir Ali the most noticeable things on the flat grey landscape, apart from the minarets of the mosques, are the pumping machines and electric wires of the wells.

The people of Pir Ali lead hard lives, and the country they live in is monotonous. The houses, which are built of mud bricks, are dull grey and white. They have only one storey and flat roofs on which most people sleep at night in wooden cots with wooden frames laced with string. The women, as in

The cotton plant

Picking cotton

many Muslim countries, are in purdah—which means that they have to keep to their own part of the house, and when they go out, even to draw water from the well or work in the fields, they have to wear burkhas, tent-like garments which cover them from head to toe, and no man may ever see them except their own husbands. The men work very hard in the fields with their bullocks and camels. They grow wheat and sugar cane and vegetables to feed their families, and the crop they grow to sell is cotton.

Cotton bushes are about waist high and they have pink, white, and yellow flowers. The flowers make seed-pods which explode as soon as they are ripe and let out a mass of white tufts. Women pick off the white tufts by hand into big baskets which the men carry to carts. The carts take the cotton to the ginning mills where the white fuzz is separated from the cotton seeds. The fuzz goes to the cotton factory where it is spun and woven into cloth, and the seeds, which contain oil, are crushed to extract the oil. The oil is used for cooking, and the rest is made into cattle-cake, which is good food for the bullocks.

Pir Ali has no cotton factory yet, and so the cotton is packed into bales and taken to the nearest railway station to be sent to the big cotton mills near the city of Lahore, about half-a-day's journey away. The farmers are paid cash for their cotton, so they are not too poor, although they do have to work hard.

The most important place in Pir Ali is the mosque with its tall, graceful minaret. The people are devout Muslims, and they listen to and obey their Mullah, or priest. Five times a day a call from the minaret reminds the people to pray, and then all the men, wherever they are, in the fields or factories, turn to face Mecca, the holy city of the Muslims, and kneel on their prayer mats and say a prayer to Allah. Once a year comes the holy month of Ramadan when all the people, women as well as men, eat and drink nothing at all from sunrise to sunset. Women do not go to the mosques in Muslim countries. They are not considered as important as men, and hardly any girls in West Pakistani villages go to school. In the cities life for women is now changing a great deal, but not much yet in the villages.

34 A Village in East Pakistan

A house in an East Pakistan village

THE ALI FAMILY lives in Comilla, a village on the Brahmaputra river in East Pakistan. Their house, like most of the other houses in the village, is built on a raised platform of rammed earth, so that when it rains very heavily and there are floods, the water does not come into the house. The walls of the house are made of thick bamboo mats, and the roof is thatched with layers of coconut leaves which make an excellent waterproof covering to keep the rain out. The houses of East Pakistan, which are called bashas, are wonderfully cool inside because the bamboo mats let air pass through the walls. As the weather in Comilla is very hot and also often very wet, the important thing is to have a house which is both cool and rainproof.

A basha is divided into rooms by bamboo partitions which do not go all the way up to the roof. All the animals of the Ali household live in the same house as the family. The hen house is perched on a bamboo pole in the kitchen; the goats and the ducks share the room where the Alis sleep and where they store rice in giant pots of baked clay.

Mahommed Ali is a peasant who has a very small plot of land on the edge of the mighty Brahmaputra river, and he is very poor. He grows rice to feed his family, and he also grows jute to sell (Chapter 35). He has built a raft of bamboo poles tied together with rough ropes made of the fibre of dried coconut husks. When he is not busy in his rice fields, looking after his jute, or mending the roof of his basha, he earns a few rupees by ferrying people or goods across the Brahmaputra. To cross the river he lets his raft drift downstream, pushing it with a long bamboo pole so that it gradually crosses over to the other side. The crossing may take as much as a whole morning, for the river is very wide. Then Mahommed Ali has to haul the raft some way upstream so that he can drift it downstream and across to get home. If there is enough wind, he hauls a rough sail onto a bamboo pole and lets the wind help him cross. When the wind helps, Mahommed Ali says an extra little prayer to thank Allah for the wind.

Amina, Mahommed Ali's wife, also tries

to earn a little money by keeping hens and selling their eggs in the market. Unlike the Muslim women in West Pakistan villages, Amina does not have to go about in a burkha, and she is treated like an equal by her husband, for there is very little purdah in East Pakistan.

The people of Comilla catch and eat a good deal of fish, especially the delicious hilsa which they bake in a mixture of oil and mustard seeds. The river is very important to the people of Comilla. They travel on the river for there are very few roads and hardly any railways. People travel in steamers, by ferries, in launches, sailing boats, or flat-bottomed boats made out of burnt-out tree trunks, or on crude rafts like Mahommed Ali's. The flat-bottomed boats are guided, like punts, with a pole and a paddle, and they are very useful for getting about from village to village. Almost all the villages in East Pakistan are either on the river or on water channels running from the river, so one can go almost everywhere by flat boats or rafts, and there is hardly any need for roads.

One very big problem in East Pakistan, as it is in Bengal (see Chapter 23), is to keep the waterways and the ponds and the tanks free from being choked up by the water hyacinth. This plant, with its pretty pale-mauve flower, has a leafy stem and deep roots, and it spreads so quickly that, unless the villagers are pulling it out all the time, it covers up the ponds and tanks and chokes the rivers so that boats cannot get along them. Everyone, even the children, has to help in getting rid of the water hyacinths.

Because it is a warm climate and there is so much water, many lovely flowers grow in East Pakistan, especially many different kinds of orchids, flowering trees, and climbing plants such as the trumpet-shaped blue or pink Morning Glory and the purple Bougainvillia. There are also tigers, snakes, and stinging scorpions in the forests, and crocodiles in the rivers.

Most of their supplies are brought to the towns and villages by river

35 Rice and Jute

BESIDES TEA, RICE and jute are the two main crops which the farmers of East Pakistan grow. Every farmer grows rice to provide food for his family. Some farmers grow more than they need and sell some to the cities, but most grow just enough for themselves. Jute they grow to sell. It is what we call a cash crop for it brings the farmer cash.

Rice is grown in all monsoon countries (see Chapter 18), wherever the climate is warm enough and there is enough water. When it is growing in the fields it is called 'paddy'. In Pakistan and India it is usually grown in small fields by the peasants. The paddy fields are small because rice crops take a lot of hard work. A small field is all one family can manage, and in good years it produces enough rice to feed one family. All goes well if it is a good season, but if the monsoon fails and there is not enough water to make the rice grow, the family is faced with starvation.

Rice is a kind of grass, and its seed-heads look rather like very large drooping grass seed-heads. It is sown fresh every time and takes a few months to grow and be ready to harvest. The farmer plants his field after the monsoon rains have started, in June or July, so that the paddy can grow during the wet season, and ripen and be harvested in the dry season. When it is ripe, it may be about 4 feet tall and golden brown, and it looks not unlike a field of ripe oats. When it is young it is very green indeed.

The farmer has to prepare his paddy field very carefully. He ploughs it thoroughly with ploughs pulled by bullocks or water buffaloes. Then he builds a little wall of earth, called a bund, round it to keep in the water when he floods it. In the meantime he sows the rice seed in a 'nursery' of soft mud. In about 6 weeks, when the bright green seedlings are about 12 inches long, he floods the field from the irrigation canals to soak the ground. Now comes the planting time when everyone in the family has to help. They all start in a row across the field, with bare feet. They move across the field, nearly up to their knees in mud and water, planting the seedlings in rows. They take two or three seedlings in one hand, make a hole in the mud with a finger, and plant the seedlings in little bunches about 8 or 10 inches apart.

As the water sinks into the ground, more water is put on the field, for the seedlings must stay in water until they have grown strong and have begun to turn a deeper green. While the crop is growing, the field has to be kept clear of weeds. Then, when the rice flowers turn to seed and the blades begin to go yellow, the water is gradually drained off the field by making a little hole in the earth wall or bund. The paddy is perhaps 3 or 4 feet high when it is ripe and ready to harvest. It is cut by hand with sharp, curved

Rice

Women husking rice

sickles, and threshed by being beaten with sticks to get the grain out of the heads. Then the farmer usually stores it in great jars, and only husks it as it is needed. To remove the husks, the grain is put in a hollow wooden log or a baked clay container and pounded with a wooden pounder. This takes off much of the husk, but leaves some behind. If the rice is sent to the factory, it is husked in steel rollers which take off much more husk, and the rice ends white, as we know it. The home-husked rice which the Indians and Pakistanis eat is much more nourishing than the factory white rice, because much of the best part of the rice is taken away with the husk. Unfortunately people in India and Pakistan, especially in the cities, are now beginning to prefer white rice, and so their food is not so nourishing as it used to be.

Jute is what we call a fibre crop—that is, it is grown for the fibres in its stems, which are woven into a very coarse sackcloth or spun into ropes. Much of the world's supply of jute comes from East Pakistan, where the hot, wet climate suits it.

The farmer sows it very thickly in his field so that the plants will grow close together, and the tall green stalks will have no side branches. Jute grows up to 10 or 12 feet tall. When it is golden brown and ready to harvest, the men either pull it up by the roots or cut it with sharp knives close to the ground, and tie it up into bundles. Then the jute has to be 'retted'—that is left to lie in shallow water until it is soft enough for the fibres in the stems to be easily separated from the pulp. Then the fibre is pressed into bales, which are piled up on to barges and taken by river to the jute mills.

In old days all the jute grown in Pakistan and north India used to be sent by sea to factories in other countries, especially to Dundee in Scotland, where it was manufactured. But today both Pakistan and India have their own jute factories, which makes the jute much more profitable for them. The sackcloth and hessian made from jute are the materials used more than anything else for packing things in. Sacks are made for holding cement, coal, potatoes, and many other things; jute cloth is used for packing machine tools and parts of machinery, for wrapping round pipes and tanks to prevent them from freezing, for making containers for storing flour, sugar, and other foods, and for making floor coverings and lining linoleum. Hessian is also used as cheap curtain material and chair coverings. The Indians have made a coarse cloth out of jute for several hundreds of years. Now it is used all over the world for all these different purposes.

Harvesting jute

36 Nepal and the Himalayas

A Nepalese band. These huge horns, which are very difficult to blow, are used at festivals

THE KINGDOM OF Nepal lies between India and Tibet, among the Himalayan mountains. Except for the plains next to India, Nepal is a mountainous country, even the valleys and lower mountain slopes being far higher than the highest mountain in Britain. The tallest mountain in the world, Mount Everest, is in Nepal, and there are several other mountains nearly as high. When mountaineers try to climb Mount Everest, they use the Sherpas, the sturdy and rugged people who live in these mountains, as porters and guides.

A long time ago the Sherpas crossed over the mountains from Tibet and settled along the southern slopes of the Himalayas in Nepal, and so they are rather like the people of Tibet to look at. In such a rugged and windswept country life is hard, and all the family, even the children, have to work if the family is to get enough to eat.

Some Sherpa families have three houses, one house on the lower slopes, one rather higher, and one very high indeed. The houses are in little village groups of seldom more than forty or fifty. Round each group of houses there are cultivated fields, usually built in narrow terraces up the hillsides. In the highest fields the Sherpas grow potatoes; in the lower fields they grow barley; and turnips, garlic, and other vegetables in the lowest ones. They also graze their yaks on the higher mountain slopes in the summer and on the lower slopes in the winter. Yaks are very hardy, large cattle, with thick hairy blackish-brown coats and long horns. The Sherpas use them for almost everything they need. They ride them, plough with them, and use them to carry their goods. They weave their hairy wool into cloth and use their hides for leather boots and tents. They milk them and get fat and meat from them. They even dry their dung and use it for fuel instead of wood or coal.

Sherpa houses are made of grey stones with dark wooden beams and shutters to the small windows, and they all look much alike. As the winds are bitter, the shutters are usually kept closed, for it is very important to keep out the cold. The animals live on the ground floor, and the people above them. There is no chimney, and the smoke has to find its way out through the wooden beams in the roof, leaving a great deal of soot behind it. The only gay things in a Sherpa village are the fluttering white prayer flags which fly from bamboo poles over the roofs of the houses. The Sherpas are Buddhists, and they believe that these prayer flags will keep away the evil eye, of which all Buddhists in Nepal are very much afraid. They also paint giant eyes on each side of the temple spires, and the monks help to keep away the evil eye by fantastic dances, for which they wear terrifying devil masks.

There are practically no roads in the Himalayas, and everything has to be carried either on yak or mule back or on human backs. Even children learn to carry heavy loads in large cone-shaped wicker baskets which are tied to them by a band which crosses over the forehead. The baskets are big enough to carry a person, and it is not uncommon to see a man carrying a sick or old person on his back in one of these baskets and climbing up or down steep paths and over mountain ridges from one valley to the next. The Sherpas are very sure-footed and think nothing of crossing a mountain torrent or a deep crevasse by balancing on a single tree trunk.

The highest ridges and peaks of the Himalayas are bleak and covered with snow, but lower down there are alpine flowers in the spring and summer, and there are fir trees. There are wonderful butterflies, kites and eagles in the skies, and black and red Himalayan bears hiding in the rocks. Rather lower still in the warmer river valleys are splendid tall evergreen oaks and chestnuts and magnificent rhododendrons and orchids.

The biggest Sherpa village is Namche Bazar, and that has only about 80 houses in it. There is a Buddhist temple and a little monastery, in the courtyard of which one of the monks holds a school. Most of the villages have no school. There is no shop or market. The Sherpas buy or sell very little, for they grow or make nearly everything they need. If they buy anything from a neighbour they pay for it by exchanging it for something else or by working a certain number of hours for the neighbour. The only thing they have to buy is salt, and perhaps some sugar and dyes, and these they buy from merchants bringing caravans of yaks over the mountains from Tibet into Nepal, and they pay for them with turnips or potatoes, which they usually slice and dry in the sun so that they are lighter to carry.

Though they have a hard life in their magnificent country, these small, sturdy, dark-haired people are nearly always cheerful, and like most Buddhist people, they are friendly and kind.

A Sherpa and yaks

37 The Valley of Katmandu

THE VALLEY OF Katmandu, which is in the heart of the kingdom of Nepal, used to be a great lake thousands of years ago. According to a Hindu legend, the god Vishnu took his mighty sword and cut a hole through the mountains so that all the water in the lake could drain away and people could come and live in the valley. The plain, which was once the bed of the lake, is very fertile and is watered by a small river, which runs down the valley and finally finds its way into the great Ganges river. The valley is protected from fierce winds and snowstorms by the high mountains to the north. It is the richest and most pleasant part of Nepal. The word Katmandu means a 'wooden bridge', and Katmandu, the capital city of Nepal, was built where once an old wooden bridge had crossed the river.

The two most important tribes of people in this small mountain kingdom are the Sherpas whom we read about in the last chapter; and the Gurkhas. The Sherpas live in the mountains towards the east and are Buddhists. The Gurkhas, who are Hindus, are the ruling people, and the kings and prime ministers of Nepal have come from Gurkha families for hundreds of years. The Gurkhas are some of the best soldiers in the world. Both when Britain ruled India and ever since they have been some of the finest soldiers in the British army.

Nepal is a kingdom, ruled by a king. The people believe that their king is a god; they think he is the god Vishnu come to live on earth, and that therefore they must obey him. The people of Nepal have a very strange custom. As well as their king, they choose a little girl who is called the Kumari, which means 'princess', and they treat her as a queen and a goddess. This little girl must be quite perfect. She must be beautiful and must have no mark on her skin, no scar or mole. When it is necessary to choose a new Kumari, all the suitable little girls of one year old are put together in a huge, very dark room in a dark palace. Then terrible noises are made in the dark, and whichever little girl shows no fear and does not cry out is considered to be divine and is chosen as the Kumari. She is taken to live in a beautiful palace in the centre of the city, where she has many servants and is looked after by the priests. Her mother and also her sisters and brothers may go with her, but no grown-up men may come near her. Every year she is beautifully dressed with rich jewellery and is taken in a procession in a gilded chariot through the streets of Katmandu to the Monkey Gate (Hanuman Doka), where she blesses the king and wishes him a prosperous year. But as soon as the little girl shows any mark on her skin, or her first teeth begin to come out, so that she is no longer perfect, she ceases to be the Kumari, and another little girl is chosen instead.

The city of Katmandu is a very beautiful capital. It is situated in the lovely fertile valley surrounded by very high mountains on which there is always snow. During much of the year there is bright sun and clear blue skies. The city has fine white marble palaces which were copied from the grand Palace of Versailles near Paris. One of the palaces built for one of the prime ministers has as many as a thousand rooms. As well, there is a splendid Buddhist temple with a spire with a golden tip and four pairs of painted eyes looking out over the country in all directions and warding off the 'evil eye' from the city.

The valley itself has splendid forests with fir trees sometimes as high as 80 or 90 feet. Every bit of land possible is cultivated. In the valley there are rice fields with their little earth walls (bunds) round them to hold in the water. Up the hillsides are terraced fields growing maize and fruit trees. In the forests near the Indian border there are tigers, leopards, elephants, and rhinoceroses, and in the hills deer, bears, and wild yaks.

The people of Nepal, whether Hindu or Buddhist, are very religious. The Buddhists are proud to remember that Buddha was born in Nepal (see Chapter 6). In the Katmandu valley, any Hindu who, even by accident, were to kill a sacred cow might lose his own life, and no Brahmin would be condemned to death whatever crime he had committed. Brahmins in Nepal today are above the law, as they used to be in India.

A Buddhist temple in the valley of Katmandu

38 Ceylon

CEYLON IS ONE of the most beautiful countries in the world. The people of Ceylon sometimes call it by an old name which means 'Golden Island'. It is rather smaller than Scotland and has about the same number of people. It lies to the south of India and, since it lies not very far north of the Equator, it is very hot, and there is not much difference between summer and winter. Also, since very heavy rains fall during the monsoon periods, a considerable part of Ceylon has a hot, damp climate where forests grow very thick. In many parts of the island, the jungle is so dense that a man cannot walk through it without cutting a path for himself with a kind of knife. There is a great deal of hilly and mountainous country where many people live, though the majority of people live near the coasts. Today there are good roads and railways, so it is quite easy to get about.

The people of Ceylon came to the island, mostly from India, at different times. The very earliest people are called the Vedda. Most of these are now farmers and fishermen, but small family parties of them still live in the jungle in the same way as they always have, almost like animals. They live in caves, hunt with bows and arrows, gather roots, wild fruit, and honey, and wear practically no clothes. Many people from northern India came to settle in Ceylon about 540 B.C., and they brought the teachings of the Buddha with them (see Chapter 6). These people are called Singhalese for that is the name of their language, and they are still Buddhists. Later, people called Tamils came over from South India, and they were Hindus. Most of the people, whether they are Hindus or Buddhists, share many of the same legends, and so most children of Ceylon would know the legend of Rama and Sita and how the monkey people helped to rescue Sita from the Devil who had taken her to Lanka, the Hindu name for Ceylon (see Chapter 3).

Today Buddhism is the most important religion, and Buddhist festivals are the holidays in Ceylon. There are many Buddhist temples, and some of the ancient ones have got lost and overgrown in the jungle. The most famous is the Temple of the Tooth, where it is believed that one of the Buddha's teeth has been preserved. This is at Kandy, the old capital of Ceylon in the centre of the island. The capital now is Colombo, a modern city and a port on the coast. Every August the Holy Tooth is taken in procession round Kandy, carried on the temple's sacred elephant. After the elephant come dancers and drummers, and then comes a procession of fifty or sixty elephants ridden by priests in magnificent robes. Like most Buddhist festivals, this takes place by moonlight.

The Buddhist New Year is a time for

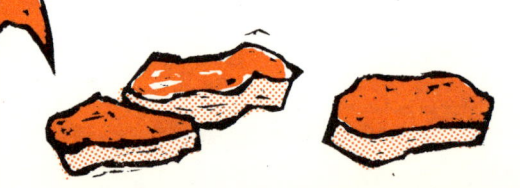

A giant Monitor

festivals and holidays. The priests and monks, with their shaven heads and saffron yellow robes, come down from Kandy to the streets of Colombo and dance the Devil's Dance to drive the evil spirits away, much as the Sherpas do in Nepal (see Chapter 36). The dancers wear brightly-painted wooden masks in fantastic shapes and colours, and they dance to the music of cymbals and horns and drums and bells, by the light of flaming torches.

Round much of the coast there is flat, very fertile land which is much like the Kerala coast (see Chapter 27). The people grow rice and coconuts and they go fishing in little boats with large three-cornered sails. Further inland in the hilly country coconuts, bananas, oranges and lemons, pineapples, and many other tropical fruits such as mangoes and paw-paws are grown, and also rubber trees. Rather higher still come the tea gardens, the most important crop in Ceylon (see Chapter 39).

In the forests are wild elephants, leopards, crocodiles, monkeys, many kinds of snakes, magnificent birds such as parakeets, golden orioles, flamingoes, and other rare birds which are hardly seen anywhere else. A strange animal is the giant monitor, a kind of lizard about 8 feet long and very heavy. It has strong claws and can climb very well. In old days, when soldiers were trying to climb the walls of a fortified town, they would tie a rope round one of these great lizards and train it to climb the wall, dragging the rope with it. Then a soldier would climb the rope after the lizard.

In the centre of Ceylon there are mountain peaks. Mount Pedro is twice as high as the highest British mountain, and Adam's Peak is nearly as high. On the top of Adam's Peak is a great rock with a mark on it which looks like the imprint of an enormous foot. According to the legend this is the mark of the Buddha's foot when he leapt from the rock into the air and was carried to Heaven.

A dancer wearing a Snake Devil mask

39 A Tea Plantation in Ceylon

MOST OF THE tea we drink comes from India or Ceylon. The Chinese have grown and drunk tea for more than 2,000 years, and the first tea drunk in Britain came from China; though only wealthy people drank it. Then the East India Company began to plant large tea plantations in parts of India to send to Britain, where it became very popular. By the end of the nineteenth century British tea-planters began to grow tea in Ceylon too, and now Ceylon makes most of her money from her tea gardens, and grows more tea than any other country, except India.

Tea needs a warm, damp climate, with rain most of the year round. Also it needs a rich deep soil, for it sends down deep roots. In Ceylon, in the hills about 2,000 to 5,000 feet above sea level, there are just the right conditions. At first people started growing coffee, not tea, in Ceylon, and the coffee bushes grew well. The early farmers cleared the forest and rooted up the trees and made more and more coffee plantations. They had to work very hard and against many difficulties. Sometimes thousands of big jungle rats would invade an estate with flourishing young coffee plants, and in a single night eat up every plant. Sometimes wild elephants would charge over an estate and trample down the crop.

Just when the coffee plantations were doing very well and the planters were making fortunes, a terrible disease attacked the coffee crops. Many planters gave up in despair and left Ceylon, but others started to plant tea instead. In particular, a man called James Taylor who had learned all he could about how to grow and manufacture tea in Assam in northern India, dug up and burnt all his coffee plants and planted tea instead. Soon he had fine tea gardens; and others with his help and advice began to do the same.

The tea James Taylor and his friends grew comes from a tree which grows wild in Assam and grows as high as 30 or 40 feet. But in the tea garden the plant is never allowed to grow tall; it is pruned so that it makes a spreading shrub about $3\frac{1}{2}$ feet high which is easy to pick from the ground. Tea-growing is very hard work, and the work goes on all the year through, for Ceylon does not have seasons as we have. Therefore all the time there are some fields ready for picking, some being planted, other being pruned, and weeding and manuring go on all the time. Also there is always work keeping the jungle back and clearing the roads and paths through the tea gardens so that trucks can get through to collect the harvest to take to the factory.

Every tea estate has a nursery where the seedlings for new tea bushes are grown in a damp shady place. When the seedlings are about 12 inches high, they are planted out every 2 feet in straight rows 4 feet apart. It takes them about 6 years to be fully grown, by which time they have spread out until from a distance they look like a thick, bright-green carpet spreading over the hills. In every tea garden pod-bearing (leguminous) shade trees are planted at intervals through the fields. These both give the tea plants shade, like large umbrellas, and their leaves and roots provide nitrogen for the soil, which tea plants need to grow well. The roots of the trees also help to stop the soil from being washed away down the hillside when the heavy rains come.

Picking tea is called 'plucking', and when the tea bushes are ready for plucking they are called 'in flush'. The plucking is done mainly by women, and very gay they look in their green, yellow, orange, or blue saris with white head-cloths, moving about among the bright-green bushes. Every bush is picked over about once a fortnight. The girls pick off the young shoots—two young leaves and a bud—and throw them over their shoulders into big wicker baskets which they carry on their backs. They empty their baskets into trucks which carry them to the tea factory.

Every estate has its own factory where the tea is 'manufactured'. First it has to be 'withered' or dried, for the leaves are full of water which must be dried out. They are spread out on hessian trays, and air is blown through them. The factory is always on a hill so that there is plenty of fresh air. Then the withered leaf is put through rollers to crush and bruise it, and then it is spread out on trays in a cool damp atmosphere to ferment. This is the most important stage which may take 2 or 3 hours or a day. The experienced tea maker presses a little with his fingers, and when the leaf begins to stick together, he knows that it is ready. The leaf is then put into a drying machine for perhaps 20 minutes, after which it looks like the black tea we know. The dried tea is

Picking tea

graded and packed into special tea-chests and sent by railway or road to Colombo to be shipped overseas. The very best grade of tea comes from the high country, and the less good quality from the lower tea gardens.

Most of the workers on a tea plantation are Tamils. They probably spend all their lives on the plantation, hardly ever going anywhere else, for the estate provides them with all they need. Each family has a two-roomed hut with a piece of land on which they can grow vegetables and keep chickens. There is a co-operative store for shopping, a hospital, an estate school (most children in Ceylon, boys and girls, go to school), and sometimes, also, a Hindu temple. There are sure to be several shrines to local Hindu gods.

40 Burma and its People

Burmese people

BURMA, AS THE map on p. 1 shows, lies to the east of India and separates India from south-east Asia. In the north are high mountains stretching up to Tibet, and the very south is a long tongue of land reaching as far south as Malaysia and not very far from the Equator. Burma is a land of mountains, forests, and river valleys. In the north the forests on the mountain slopes grow splendid teak trees which are one of the riches of Burma (see Chapter 41); in the south along the coasts are swampy forest jungles. The most important river valley is that of the Irrawaddy, with its big tributary, the Chindwin (see Chapter 43), and this widens out into rich lowlands where vast quantities of rice are grown. The people of Burma grow so much rice that there is a great deal to export to other countries, such as India and China, which do not grow enough themselves for their very large populations. So the Burmese are better off than most Indians because they have enough to eat—not only rice, but fish, fruit, and coconuts.

Because of the mountains along the west, north, and east, it is much easier to reach Burma by sea than by land, and most people come to Burma by the great port of Rangoon. The teak and rice and oil which Burma sells to other countries come down the Irrawaddy river to Rangoon to be shipped. So Rangoon is a very important city with nearly a million people and a great many big business and government buildings, big oil refineries, and a university. Yet, little more than 100 years ago Rangoon was no more than a fishing village.

Burma is dependent, like India and other countries described in this book, on the monsoon rains (see Chapter 18). But most of Burma gets plenty of water, either from heavy rains or from the great rivers. This is why rice grows so well. Even in the Dry Zone in central Burma, where there is not a great deal of rain, there is plenty of water in the rivers for irrigating the fields and growing rice.

As well as all the Indians and Chinese who come to Burma to make a living, especially in business, there are many different peoples living in different parts of the country. Some of the mountain tribes in the north are more like the people of Tibet or of north-west India, and are very different from the true Burmese of the Irrawaddy plains or Rangoon.

The Nagas, most of whom belong to the Indian State of Nagaland, are a warlike people who fight with bows and arrows and perform war dances in wonderful warlike costumes. They live in large villages, often perched on a mountain ridge and protected by stockades of very sharp bamboo spikes.

These fences are not only to protect them from enemy tribes, but also from wild elephants, tigers, leopards, and other animals. The Nagas are head-hunters, for they believe that to hang the head of a victim from another village over the doorpost will bring prosperity to the hunter's village. Today, however, most Naga tribes have been converted to Christianity by missionaries, and they are learning to grow crops as well as to hunt and fight. Their way of farming is very wasteful, for they set fire to a patch of forest and then, when it rains, sow their seed in the ashes. But now they are learning to build terraced fields on the hillsides, to plough them properly, and to irrigate the crops.

In the hills farther south-east live the Karen people, many of whom are Christian. They had a legend that one day a man with golden hair, a face of ivory, and carrying a book would come to them, and that he would be their God. When the first British missionary arrived with fair hair, white skin, and carrying a Bible, the Karens immediately welcomed him as a god.

Most of the true Burmese people are Buddhists. In the hills to the east of Burma, through which the river Salween runs, live the Shan people. Until quite recently they ruled themselves, with princes and princesses of little states which were not much more than villages. The land is fertile, and there is plenty of water when the rains come, so the Shans grow rice in small fields in the valleys and between the patches of forest. They also mine for rubies by digging tunnels into the limestone hills and washing out the precious stones. Merchants come to the Mogok ruby mines to bargain for the rubies. The bargaining is done silently by signs and by pressing hands under a table, so that no one but the buyer and seller know what the price is.

The ruling people of Burma originally came from China and built a beautiful city called Pagan. Today this ancient capital is mostly in ruins, though there are still hundreds of Buddhist temples over this part of Burma. The great Ananda Pagoda at Pagan, which was built in 1091, is one of the most beautiful buildings in the world. Rather more than 100 years ago one of the last of the Burmese kings built a new capital at Mandalay on a bend of the Irrawaddy. He laid it out with palaces and monasteries and temples, mostly built of the beautiful hard teak wood with magnificent carvings. There were lovely gardens and bridges and terraces. Unfortunately, most of it was destroyed in the Second World War, but it is still a much more truly Burmese city than the great city of Rangoon.

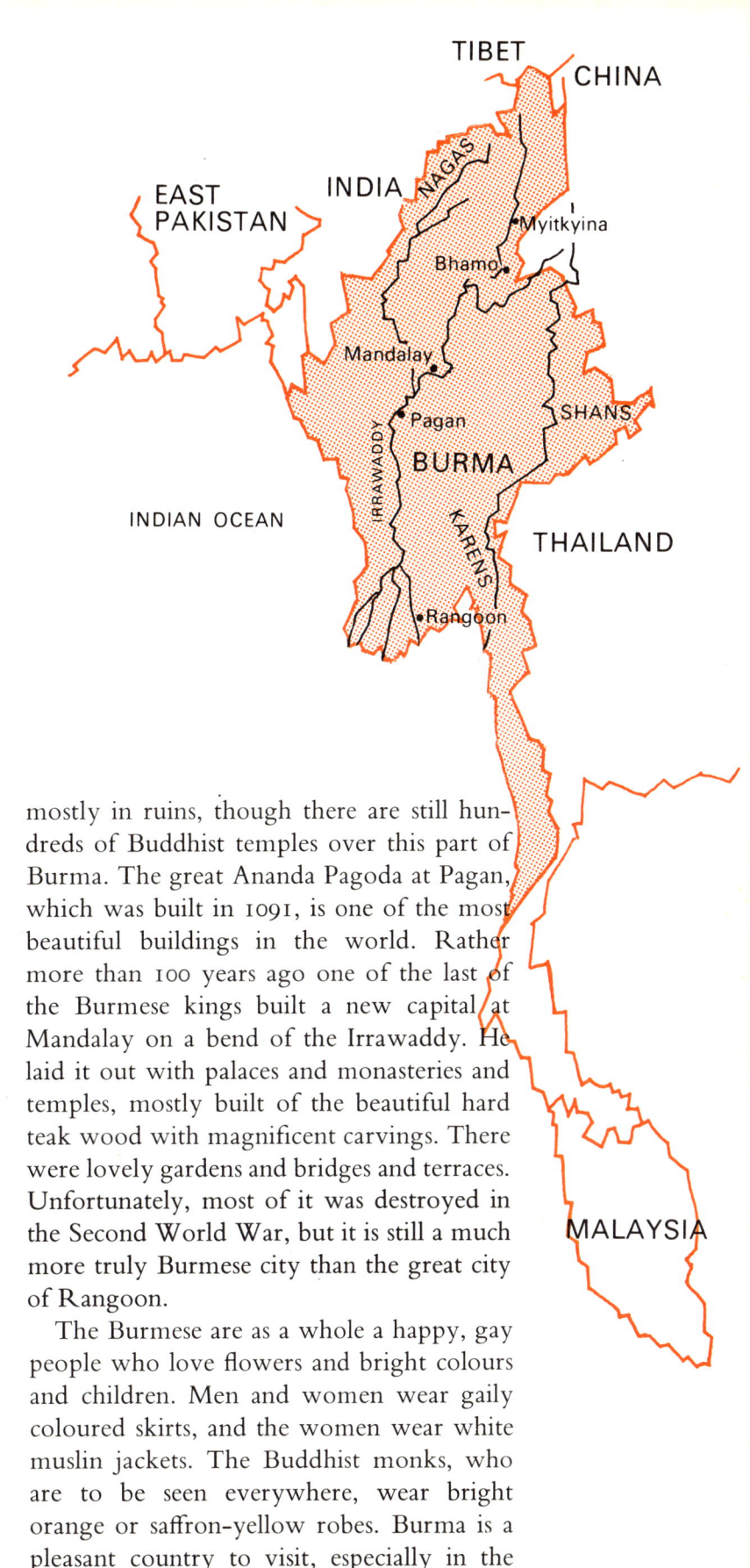

The Burmese are as a whole a happy, gay people who love flowers and bright colours and children. Men and women wear gaily coloured skirts, and the women wear white muslin jackets. The Buddhist monks, who are to be seen everywhere, wear bright orange or saffron-yellow robes. Burma is a pleasant country to visit, especially in the cool season from November to February.

41 The Teak Forests of Burma

TEAK IS A very hard timber which is particularly valuable for building ships. Some of the best teak in the world comes from the monsoon forests of Burma.

A teak tree has a tall, straight trunk with spreading branches towards the top. It grows 150 feet or more tall. It has wide leaves as much as 20 inches long and spikes of yellowish flowers. As with many trees of tropical forests, it grows very fast, perhaps several feet each year. The wood has oil in it which preserves it so that it does not rot in water or warp with old age, and it has a gum in it which stops pests such as white ants or wood worms from eating it. It is a heavy wood with a straight, even grain which makes it easy to work, and it polishes very well. Teak is so valuable to Burma that the Government owns all the teak forests, and Government foresters say which trees are to be cut and where new ones are to be planted.

In the forest the teak trees grow in small groups with perhaps not more than 10 or 12 trees to the acre. The rest of the forest consists of many kinds of smaller trees, bamboos, and a dense undergrowth of long grass, in which tigers and many other wild animals live. The country is so steep, with so many deep river gorges running through it, that it is almost impossible to build roads through it. So the teak trunks, after they have been felled, are dragged to the banks of the nearest river and floated out of the forests and down to the saw-mills. The foresters make tracks for themselves and their elephants through the jungle, and the people who live in villages in clearings in the forest make swinging bridges over the river gorges with bamboos and ropes.

When a tree is fully grown and ready to fell, a broad ring is cut round it near the ground, which cuts away the outer sapwood. This kills the tree. Then it is left standing for as much as 3 years to dry out. If it were cut down immediately it would be much too heavy to handle and would not float, but after most of the water in it has dried away, it is not only easier to transport but it is already partly seasoned and ready for the saw-mills.

Most of the work of dragging the teak trunks to the river banks is done by elephants. The elephant's rider in Burma is called an 'oozie' and each oozie trains and looks after and works one elephant. As men and elephants live about the same length of time, a boy and an elephant often grow up together, the boy gradually teaching the elephant all he needs to learn, and they grow very devoted to each other. The elephant has to learn to kneel when told, to turn to right or left at a touch, to push and pull logs with its trunk or with chains, judging just how far to pull and how to manoeuvre the log out of the jungle and up and down steep slopes. It takes him several years to learn, and his oozie a great deal of patience. But when he is fully trained, an elephant can be very clever.

Each day when the dawn breaks, the oozie sets out from the camp to find his elephant who may have wandered several miles in search of the bamboo shoots, leaves, and grass, of which he eats about 600 pounds a day. They return together to the camp, where the oozie has his breakfast of steaming rice, and then they set off for the day's work. They bring each teak log to the river and place it so that the flood waters will float it and carry it down the stream. Then they return to the camp, and the elephant, with his rear legs hobbled so that he cannot wander too far, is turned out to find his food. In the 2 or 3 months of the hot, dry season when the teak trees have shed most of their leaves and give no protection from the blazing sun, the elephants do no work. They need all their time for finding themselves enough green stuff to eat.

In the meantime the foresters have to see that the river courses are clear of rocks so that when the rains come, the logs can be carried down the streams. When the logs are floating down, they have to look out that they do not get stuck and to release them if they jam—a very difficult and dangerous task.

Most of the teak logs are floated to the Irrawaddy and then, tied together in big rafts, they are floated down to the saw-mills at Mandalay, where they are dried and cut into convenient lengths for being sent by ship to other countries. Some are taken right on to the saw-mills at Rangoon.

Elephants carrying logs in a teak forest

42 Phek, a Burmese Village

U BA AND DAW SA live in a village in central Burma in what is called the Dry Zone. U means 'Uncle' and Daw means 'Aunt', and in Burma these words are used as we use Mr. and Mrs. They are terms of respect, and children always use them when speaking to their parents. In Burma, however, a woman keeps her own name when she marries instead of taking her husband's name. This is because in Burma women are treated with great respect and are considered just as important as men.

The village of Phek, which is like countless other villages in Burma, lies beside one of the many streams which flow through the hills and across the plains to the river Irrawaddy. The stream is very important to the villagers for it brings them water, it provides them with fish, and they use it instead of a road for travelling by. In this part of Burma much less rain falls than in most parts, which is why it is called the Dry Zone. From November to February the weather is lovely—not too hot and with clear sunny skies. Then it begins to get hotter and hotter. The sun blazes down, and everywhere is brown and dusty, and a purple haze

A woman weaving cloth in a Burmese village

hangs over the country. At last, about June, the rains come in violent thunderstorms. But they are so violent that they turn everything into mud and wash away the good soil and do more harm than good. Apart from these terrific storms, not a great deal of rain falls, even at this time of year. The villagers depend much more on irrigation than rain for watering their crops. They build little dams across the streams and make artificial lakes to preserve the water which comes rushing down from the hills after the storms. Also they dig deep wells in the sandy soil. They make irrigation canals to the fields, and in this way there is generally enough water to grow plenty of rice. They also grow other crops such as millet, so that they are certain of food even if water runs short and the rice fails.

U Ba, Daw Sa, and their son Tin Tot and his sister live in a house which is built on stilts, like almost all village houses in Burma. This means that when thunderstorms flood the land, the house is safe and dry. The house has a wooden framework, and the walls and floor are of bamboo. The roof is thatched with palm leaves, and it juts out over the walls to give shade or to carry the rainwater away from the house. The house usually has only one long room in which the family live, cook, eat, and sleep. It is dark inside and the smoke from the fire rises to the roof and keeps off mosquitoes. There is a verandah along one side of the house, with bamboo chairs and tables. The shady part under the floor of the house makes another room where the animals live and where for a great part of the year Daw Sa sits to weave cloth and U Ba makes tools and weaves big bamboo baskets, which he lines with clay and uses to store rice and other things. There is always enough to eat for, besides millet and rice, there is fruit from the mango grove, oil from groundnuts, and fish from the river. Daw Sa dries some of the fish in the sun and then stores it against the dry season when there is little water in the stream and no fish.

Like most Burmese, U Ba and his family are afraid of snakes and dare not kill them, even poisonous cobras. There is a belief that if you kill a snake, his mate and all his fellow snakes will come and kill you in revenge. According to an old Burmese legend, there was once a queen who had a king-cobra for her lover. The cobra came to her room every night disguised as a man. When the queen's ministers began to urge her to marry, she promised to marry any man who could sleep in her palace for one night. Many suitors came, but every night the king-cobra killed them, and they were found dead in their beds in the morning. Then came one suitor who, instead of getting into his bed, put the trunk of a banyan tree into the bed, and himself, armed with a sword, hid nearby to watch. Soon the king-cobra slid into the room and up to the bed and bit the dummy in the bed. Instantly the man sprang out and slew the cobra with his sword. Ever since, cobras and all other snakes are supposed to kill those who kill snakes.

U Ba, like other Burmese, is a Buddhist and very religious. Spirits play an important part in people's lives. The spirits are usually friendly if they are treated properly, but no one dare offend them. Every village has its Buddhist temple or pagoda, with its roof curled up at the corners. A grand pagoda has several roofs all curled up and looking not unlike a wedding cake. There are usually several little shrines as well for local spirits, often built near a spreading banyan tree, where there is a shelter and a large jar of water so that travellers may rest and refresh themselves.

A Burmese pagoda

43 The River Irrawaddy

A boatman on the Irrawaddy

THIS GREAT RIVER runs for 1,300 miles from the very north of Burma, right through the centre of the country, to the sea near the city of Rangoon. The life of Burma has always depended on the river. Not only does it supply water all through the year, but for a long time it was the only highway through the country. Steamers can travel up the river for more than 900 miles, and most goods are carried by water. There is a railway now running from Rangoon to Mandalay and up to the town of Myitkyina (pronounced mit-chi-nar), but it is far cheaper to carry goods by water.

Many thousands of years ago Burma was quite different from what it is now. The whole centre of the country was a great arm of the sea running up between the mountains, and the land where Rangoon now stands was not there at all. Year by year, all through the centuries, as the river rushes down from the mountains it brings with it great quantities of mud, called silt. As it reaches the flatter lands and begins to flow more slowly, it drops some of the silt, but most of it is carried to the sea where it builds up mud banks. As more and more silt was brought down by the river, the mud built up islands in the sea, and then filled up the channels between the islands, pushing the land out into the sea. Every year the Irrawaddy silt builds up another 60 yards or so of land.

Today, the river breaks into many branches which find their way to the sea between the mud banks. This is called the Delta, and the land between the branches of the river is a sea of bright-green rice fields. Some of the branches are dredged and kept clear of mud so that the big ships can go up them, especially to Rangoon, which is now nearly 20 miles from the sea. In another several thousand years Rangoon may be an inland town.

The Irrawaddy starts as two mountain torrents high up near the frontier of Tibet. These rivers force their way through the mountains and forests in deep rocky gorges which the mountain people cross by flimsy swinging foot bridges made of ropes and bamboos. Where the two rivers meet, the real Irrawaddy begins. There is so much water that the river is already at places a quarter of a mile wide, but at other places it passes through narrow gorges where all this water has to force its way through a gap perhaps only 50 yards wide and many miles long, with high cliffs on each side In the dry season small steamers can travel from Myitkyina to Bhamo, but the bigger ships start from Bhamo.

It takes about 4 days to travel by steamer from Bhamo to Mandalay. Except for another gorge called the 'Gates of the Irrawaddy', the river flows more smoothly with hills on either side. It passes through patches of forest and stretches of rice fields in the valley and terraces up the hillsides. In the dry season they are brown and dusty; in the growing season they are vivid green; and as the rice ripens they turn golden-brown. On the side of the river are stacks of teak logs waiting to be floated down to the Mandalay saw-mills.

By the time the Irrawaddy reaches Mandalay, which is situated on the east bank, it is about a mile wide—wider in the wet season and narrower in the dry. There is no bridge across it—in fact, there is only one bridge over the Irrawaddy before it reaches Rangoon, and that is a modern steel railway bridge just south of Mandalay. Everyone crosses the river by ferry. It is very difficult to build bridges over a river which may become nearly 2 miles wide in time of flood.

It takes nearly a week to travel from Mandalay to Rangoon, and the steamer calls at many river ports on the way. As life is centred on the river, there are gay riverside markets and a great variety of boats, from big steamers to rafts and square-sailed junks and little boats with fishermen throwing out their great fishing nets. Back from the river on rising ground stand the villages, each one with its pagoda. Between Mandalay and Pagan the Chindwin joins the Irrawaddy, and together they flow on smoothly, winding across the plain until the river divides into the many branches of the Delta.

As the steamer comes near Rangoon, the great Shwedagon Pagoda, the largest pagoda in the world, can be seen rising from a hill beside the city. This splendid Buddhist temple, built more than 1,300 years ago, is the pride of all Buddhists of Burma. Its many pinnacles and curved roofs are covered with gold and studded with precious stones which glitter in the sun like something out of a fairy tale. The coast south of Rangoon is a swampy jungle, the home of crocodiles, which is gradually getting filled up with silt and pushed out into the sea.

The Shwedagon Pagoda in Mandalay

INDEX

Adam's Peak, Ceylon, 83
Ajanta, Buddhist monastery, 20
Akbar, Mogul Emperor of India, 26
Allah, God of Islam, 24, 73
Amritsar temple, 29
Ananda Pagoda, Buddhist temple, 87
ancient India, 10
animals: of the jungle, 44, 83; domestic, 59, 74, 78 89; sacred, 11, 13, 23; animal legends, 12, 91
architecture: ancient India, 10; under Rajputs, 23; under Moguls, 27; see also cities; temples
Arcot, 32
Ashoka, Indian Emperor, 20
Assam: map, 9; tea-growing, 84; game sanctuary, 45

Babur, Turkish (Mogul) invader of India, 26
bananas, 60, 83
bazaars, markets, 64, 69
bears, 79
Benares, Indian sacred city, 56
Bengal, Indian province, 31; village in, 52
Bhagiratha, legendary king, 57
Bhakra Dam, 62
birds, 44, 79, 83; legendary bird, 13
'Black Hole of Calcutta', 33
boats, 57, 75, 83, 92
Bombay, Indian province, 31; city, 65
Brahmaputra River, India and East Pakistan, 8, 74
Brahmins, Hindu priests, 16, 36, 81
bridges and ferries, 43, 57, 89; Howrah Bridge, 57
British rule in India, 31, 32, 34, 36, 38
Buddha, the founder of Buddhism, 18
Buddhism, 20; in Nepal, 78, 80; in Ceylon, 82; in Burma, 87, 91, 93
bullocks, 46, 58, 76; in festivals, 59; see also cattle
Bulls, Festival of, 59
burkha, Muslim woman's costume, 67
Burma, 86–92; map, 8

Calcutta, Indian city, 31, 33, 57, 65
camels, domestic, 51, 67, 69, 73
caravan trade, 69, 79
cashew nuts, 61
caste system, 16, 23, 34, 36
castor oil, crop, 51
cattle: wild, 44; sacred, 23; see also bullocks
Cawnpore (Kanpur), 57
Ceylon, 82, 84; map, 8
Cherrapunji, north-east India, 43
children in India, 34, 46, 49, 52, 61; Sherpas, 79; Pathans, 68; in Ceylon, 85; in Burma, 87, 89
chillies, see spices
Chindwin, river in Burma, 86, 93
Chotagaon, Indian village in the Deccan, 58
cities: in India, 64; in Pakistan, 67; in Nepal, 80; in Ceylon, 82; in Burma, 86, 92

climate, 8; monsoon, 42; Ceylon, 82; Burma, 90; see also rainfall
Clive, Robert, British governor, 32
clothes, see costume
cobras, snakes, 44, 91
coconuts, 52, 53, 60, 83
coffee plantations, 84
coir, coconut fibre, 60
Colombo, city in Ceylon, 82
costume: Hindu, 21, 50, 60; Muslim, 29, 66; Ceylon, 85; Burma, 87
cotton, 73, 59, 65
crane, bird, 44
crocodiles, 44, 75, 83, 92
crops: coconuts, 60; cotton, 73, 59; jute, 76; millet, 46, 59; rice, 76, 92; sugar, 59; tea, 84; wheat, 54

Dacca, city in Pakistan, 67
dams, 62, 71
dances: Buddhist, 79, 83: Punjabis, 55
Deccan, Indian plateau, 58
deer, 44, 81; in legend, 12
Delhi, Indian city: under the Sultans, 25; under the Moguls, 26, 28; modern, 64
Devil's Dance, Buddhist ceremony, 83
dhoti, Pakistan male costume, 66
Draupadi, Indian legendary queen, 14
Durga, Hindu goddess, 53

East India Company, 30, 32, 34, 65
education: India, 47, 61, 62; Pakistan, 73; Nepal, 79; Ceylon, 85
egret, bird, 44
electricity, generating of, 62, 71
elephants: wild, 44, 80; for work, 88; in processions, 41, 82
Everest, Mount, 78
evil eye, Buddhist belief, 79

factories, see industry
family life, see village life
famine, 43, 76
fertilizers, manufacture of, 63
festivals: in India, 12, 53, 59, 61; in Nepal, 80; in Ceylon, 82
flamingo, bird, 83
floods and flood control, 42, 56, 70
flowers, wild, 9, 75, 79
food: India, 47, 49, 53, 59, 61; Pakistan, 67, 69, 75, 77; Nepal, 78; Ceylon, 83; Burma, 86, 91
forests: Nepal, 80; Ceylon, 82; Burma, 86, 88; animals of, 44
Fort St. David, 32
French traders, in India, 31, 32
fruit crops, 60, 69, 83
funeral customs, see suttee

game sanctuaries, 45
Gandhi, Mahatma, Indian leader, 37, 38

94

Ganesh, Hindu god, 23, 59
Ganga, legendary maiden, 57
Ganges River, 56
Gautama (the Buddha), 18
Ghazni, Mahmud of, Afghanistan warrior-prince, 24
government: India under Rajputs, 22; under Muslim Emperors, 25; under British, 36; Independent India, 40; Independent Pakistan, 66; Nepal, 80
groundnuts, 54
Gujerat, sultan of, 28
gur, unrefined sugar, 59
Gurkhas, people of Nepal, 80

Hanuman, Hindu god, 13
Hawkins, Captain William, British trader, 30
Himalaya Mountains, 78; *map*, 9; legend, 57
Hindu gods: *see* Shiva; Durga; Ganesh; Hanuman; Ravana; Vishnu
Hinduism, 16, 23; *see also* festivals; Ganges; suttee; temples
Hindustan, Muslim empire, 25
Holi festival, 55
holidays, *see* festivals
Holy Tooth Festival, Kandy, 82
Hooghly River, branch of Ganges, 57, 65
houses: Indian villages, 48, 50, 52, 54, 56, 58, 61; Pakistan 68, 72, 74; Nepal, 78; Burma, 90; *see also* cities
Howrah Bridge, Calcutta, 65
human sacrifice, 34

India: *map* 8; ancient, 10; Muslim rule, 28; British rule, 36; Independence, 40; *see also* village life; cities
Indian Mutiny, 35
Indus River, 70; valley, ancient cities of, 10
industry, 62; jute, 76; cotton, 73, 65; coconuts, 60; rice, 86; tea, 84; timber, 88; home industry, 51, 59, 91
insects, 9, 45
Irrawaddy River, Burma, 90, *map*, 9
irrigation: India, 54, 58, 63; Pakistan, 70, 72, 76; Burma, 90, 86
Islam, *see* Muslims
Islamabad, city in Pakistan, 67

jackals, 44
Jehangir, Mogul Emperor, 29, 30
jewels, in women's costume, 50; ruby mines, Burma, 87
jungle, 45; *see also* forests
jute, fibre crop, 76

Kabul, city in Afghanistan, 69
Kandy, city in Ceylon, 82
Karachi, city in Pakistan, 67
Karens, people of Burma, 87
Kashmir, *map*, 8
Katmandu, city in Nepal, 80

Kauravas, legendary kings of India, 14
Kerala, Indian state, 60
Khyber Pass, Pakistan, 69
Kumari, Nepalese 'queen', 80

Lahore, city in Pakistan, 67
languages: ancient India, 21; Bengali, 66; Malayalam, 61; Urdu, 67
Lawrence, John, British Viceroy, 35
legends and stories: Rama and Sita, 12; Mahabharata, 14; the priest, 16; Buddha, 18, 83; Durga, 52; Ganga, 57; Ganesh, 59; Katmandu, 80; Karen, 87; King Cobra, 91
leopards, 44, 80, 83
Lights Festival, 61
lizards, 83
Lloyd Barrage, on Indus River, 71

Madras, Indian province, 30; city, 32
Mahabharata, Indian story, 14
Mahatma Gandhi, *see* Gandhi
Mahmud of Ghazni, Afghanistan warrior-prince, 24
maize, cereal crop, 54, 68, 81
malaria, disease, 45
Mandalay, city of Burma, 87
mangoes, 83, 91
markets, *see*, bazaars
marriage customs: Hindu, 34, 38, 54; Muslim, 29
merchants, *see* trade
millet, cereal crop, 46, 49, 51, 90
Mogok ruby mines, 87
Mogul emperors, 26, 28
Mohammed, Muslim founder, 24; *see also* Muslims
Mohan Roy, Indian reformer, 34
Mohenjodaro, city of ancient India, 10
monkeys, 44, 83; legendary monkey people, 13
monks, Buddhist, 20, 79, 83
monsoon, rainy season, 42
Moslems, *see* Muslims
mosques, 28, 73
Muslims, followers of Mohammed, 24, 28, 73; Muslim State, *see* Pakistan

Nagas, people of north-east India and Burma, 86
Namche Bazar, Sherpa village, 79
Nanak, Sikh leader, 29
Nepal, 78, 80, *map*, 8

oil: castor oil, 50; groundnut oil, 54, 91; coconut oil, 60; cotton oil, 73
oozie, elephant rider, 89
Outcastes, in caste system, 16, 36

paddy, *see* rice
Pagan, city of Burma, 87
pagoda, Buddhist monument, 91, 93, 87
paintings: in Ajanta, 20; on houses in Rajasthan, 50
Pakistan Republic, 66; West Pakistan, 68, 72; East Pakistan, 74; *map*, 8

Palanquin, *illus.*, 36
Pandavas, legendary kings of India, 14
parakeets, birds, 83
Pathans, people of North-West Frontier, 68
Patna, 57
paw-paws, fruit, 83
peacocks, 50, 23, 44
peasants, *see* village life
peoples: of ancient India, 10; (Burma) Karens, Shans, 86, 87; (Ceylon) Vedda, Singhalese, Tamils, 82, 84; (Nepal) Sherpas, Gurkhas, 78, 80; (Pakistan) Pathans, 68; *see also* village life
peppers, *see* spices
Peshawer, city of Pakistan, 69
pigs, wild, 45
pilgrimages, 22, 57
plants, *see* crops; flowers, wild; trees
Plassey, battle of, 33
ploughing, 46, 76, 78
pottery, village craft, 52
President, ruler of India, 40
priests: Hindu, 16, 36; Muslim, 73; Buddhist, 83
princes, of India, 20, 22, 31, 41
processions, 40; *see also* festivals
Punjab: in India, 54; in Pakistan, 71
purdah, seclusion of women, 29, 50, 73

races, *see* peoples
rainfall, 8; monsoon, 42; betting on, 51
Rajasthan, Indian state, 50
Rajputs, Indian princes, 22, 41
Ram Lila Festival, 12
Ram Mohan Roy, *see* Mohan Roy
Rama and Sita, Indian legend, 12
Ramadan, Muslim fast, 73
Rangoon, city of Burma, 87, 92
Ravana, demon in Indian legend, 12
reincarnation (rebirth), 16
religions, *see* Buddhism; Hinduism; Muslims; Sikhs
Republic Day, Indian celebration, 40 rhinoceroses, 44, 81
rice: in India, 60; in Pakistan, 76; in Burma, 86
rivers, 8; Ganges, 56; Indus, 70; Brahmaputra, 74; Irrawaddy, 92; *see also* dams
rubies, mining of, 87

sacred animals, 23; legends of, 13
sacrifice, human, 34
salt, floods and evaporation, 72
Salt March (Gandhi), 38
Salween, river in Burma, 87
sari, dress of Indian women, 14, 60
schools, *see* education
sculpture, 20
sepoy, Indian soldier, *illus.*, 31
Shah Jehan, Mogul emperor, 27
Shan, people of Burma, 87
sheep: wild, 8; sheep farming, Pakistan, 69
Sherpas, people of Nepal, 78

Shiva, Hindu god, 24, 59, 57
Shwedagon Pagoda, Burma, 93
Sikhs, 29
silt, brought down by rivers, 56, 70, 92
Sindri, Indian industrial town, 63
Singhalese, people of Ceylon, 82
Sita, legendary princess, 12
slums, 65
snakes, 44, 61, 83; sacred, 53, 91
spices: trade in, 30; in food, 47, 49, 61
states of India, 64, 40
stories, *see* legends and stories
sugar cane, 58; home-made sugar, 49; *illus.*, 70
sultans, Muslim, 25
Suraj-ud-Dowlah, Indian ruler, 33
suttee, funeral custom, 23, 34, 36

Taj Mahal, 27
Tamils, people of Ceylon, 82, 85
Tatayu, legendary bird, 13
tea plantations, 84
teak trees, 88
Temple of the Tooth, Kandy, 82
tigers, 44, 81, 88
timber, Burma, 88
tools: of ancient India, 11; honouring of, at festival, 61
towns, *see* cities; village life
temples: Buddhist, 20, 87, 93; Hindu, 24; Sikh, 28
trade: in India, 30, 64; caravan trade, 69, 79; rice trade, 86; tea trade, 84
Tuglak Mohammed, Muslim general, 25

Untouchables, *see* Outcastes
Urdu, Pakistan language, 67

Vedda, people of Ceylon, 82
Viceroy, British ruler, 35, 36
village life: India, 46, 49, 50, 52, 54, 58, 60; Pakistan, 72, 74; Nepal, 78; Ceylon, 84; Burma, 90
Vishnu, Hindu god, 57, 80
vultures, 44

wars: ancient, 14, 20; of Rajput princes, 22; Muslim-Hindu, 24, 28, 39; Anglo-French, 31, 32; *see also* Indian Mutiny
water buffalo, 76
water hyacinth, 75
water supply, 50, 52, 54, 58; dams, 62, 71; *see also* irrigation
weather, *see* climate
weaving, village craft, 59; *illus.*, 90
wedding ceremonies, 54
wheat, *see* crops
women, position in society: Hindu, 22, 34, 50; Muslim, 29, 67, 73; Buddhist, 90
writing: of ancient India, 21; modern, *illus.*, 67

yaks, cattle, 78